HOUS

MW01141201

Can't Boil Water

Outskirts Press, Inc.
Denver, Colorado

Outskirts Press
http://www.outskirtspress.com

ISBN-10: 1-4327-0025-1
ISBN-13: 978-1-4327-0025-6

Outskirts Press and the "OP" logo are trademarks belonging to Outskirts Press, Inc.

Printed in the United States of America

Grandpa had a great philosophy about food.
He always said,
"If you like it, it's good for you."
"Bon Appétit."

Jo Alice & Cis

The "Can't Boil Water" cookbook contains a selection of the best recipes from the collections of the Authors. They have chosen to include those recipes that have been tested and used by many generations of family and friends. Each recipe was reviewed with the beginning cook in mind and revised and/or updated to help any cook to be successful with preparing the recipes. In addition, there are several tips throughout the book plus extra pages that will assist the beginning cook with terms as well as useful guidelines and "how to's." All tips are listed in the index on pages 198 to 200.

Please read each recipe completely before proceeding to cook. Gather all ingredients, utensils and pans, etc. before you are ready to begin. Notice that each recipe has a list of ingredients along the left side with a large bracket to the right of the list and in the center of the page, dividing the ingredients list and the instructions for that list. Be sure to follow the bracketed instructions for the list of ingredients carefully before proceeding to the main instructions that appear below each recipe.

Have fun cooking!

BREAKFAST

PAN SIZES

~ **Saucepan:** A round pan with a handle. May be purchased with or without a lid. Sizes range from 1 quart (small), 2 quart (medium), and 3 quart (large.)

~ **Skillet**: Has a flat bottom with 2" to 4" sides that are flared or sloped, which makes it easier to toss and turn food with a spatula. Recommended sizes for normal use is one 8" and one 10" non-stick surface, and a 10 1/2" cast iron. Refer to page 207 for instructions on how to "season" a cast iron skillet.

~ **Double Boiler:** Consists of two pans where one sits inside of the other. Fill the bottom pan with about 2" of water and bring to a simmer before putting top pan in place. Be careful not to let the water evaporate completely from the bottom pan or it will burn on the bottom.

~ **Dutch Oven:** A large, round pot with a lid and handles on each side. 6 quarts is a good size.

~ **Roasting Pan**: Is usually a large oval pan with a lid and holds approximately 9 quarts.

~ **Casserole Dish**: An oven proof glass or metal pan. Usually a 9" x 13" x 2" size. Oven temperature should be reduced by 25⁰ for class dishes.

~ **Cookie Sheet**: Generally, it is best to purchase one medium size (10" x 15" x 1/2" and one large size (11" x 17" x 3/4").

~ **Jellyroll Pan**: Is like a cookie sheet, but is at least 1" deep.

BACON WRAPPED EGGS

Preheat oven to 350⁰

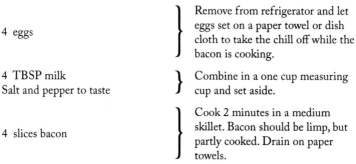

4 eggs } Remove from refrigerator and let eggs set on a paper towel or dish cloth to take the chill off while the bacon is cooking.

4 TBSP milk
Salt and pepper to taste } Combine in a one cup measuring cup and set aside.

4 slices bacon } Cook 2 minutes in a medium skillet. Bacon should be limp, but partly cooked. Drain on paper towels.

Spray four individual baking dishes with cooking spray. Circle inside of each dish with a bacon slice. Break the shell of one egg and gently drop the yolk and white into a cup then slip the egg into one dish. Repeat, using the remaining eggs and dishes. Add 1 TBSP of milk mixture to each dish. Set dishes on a medium cookie sheet or shallow pan.
Bake in a 350⁰ oven for 15 to 20 minutes or until egg is set.
Serves 4.

Can't Boil Water #1: Individual baking dishes are also named custard cups. Usually they are sold individually. The best ones are, in my opinion, stoneware. Those made of glass are best used for non-greasy baking, such as custards.

7

BAKED FRENCH TOAST

1/2 cup milk
1/2 tsp. vanilla extract
Pinch of salt
2 eggs, slightly beaten

Break each egg, one at a time, into a small cup then beat slightly. In a medium bowl, combine eggs and remaining ingredients. Stir well using a whisk.

1 cup corn flake cereal crumbs
(Can't Boil Water #34)

Place in a separate shallow bowl.

8 slices French bread

Diagonally cut into 1" thick slices.

1/4 cup butter

Melt butter in microwave (See Can't Boil Water #2 below).

Preheat oven to 450⁰.
Dip bread slices into milk mixture, then dredge (that is coat on both sides) in corn flake crumbs. Place bread slices on a baking sheet and drizzle (pour evenly) with butter.
Bake 15 minutes or until golden brown.

NOTE: French bread can be purchased sliced.

VERY GOOD SERVED WITH THE "OMELET IN A BAG" page 14.

Can't Boil Water #2: Dice butter into small pieces and drop in a glass measuring cup. Cover with a paper towel. Microwave on high 20 seconds. Repeat every 10 seconds until butter is completely melted.

BREAKFAST PIE

Preheat oven to 350⁰

CRUST:
4 biscuits, torn into small pieces
3 TBSP butter, melted
1/2 tsp. salt

Toss together in a medium bowl to combine and arrange evenly in the bottom of a 9" pie pan.

FILLING:
6 slices bacon

Cook in a medium skillet, on medium heat, until crisp or lay two paper towels on top of two thin paper plates (DO NOT use plastic or foam plates), separate bacon pieces and lay out on the top paper towel. Cover with two paper towels and microwave about 30 seconds per slice or until crisp. Drain and crumble.

8 ounces grated sharp cheddar cheese

Place in a small bowl and set aside.

3 eggs
1 1/2 cups half & half
1/2 tsp. salt
1/4 tsp. pepper

Break eggs into a medium bowl and beat slightly. Add half & half, salt and pepper. Stir well to blend.

Crumble half the bacon over the crust. Sprinkle with half of the cheese. Gently pour in the egg mixture. Top with remaining bacon and cheese.

Bake in 350⁰ oven for 40 minutes or until knife comes out clean when inserted in center of pie (Can't Boil Water #3).
Remove from oven and let cool for a few minutes before serving.

BREAKFAST PIZZA

1 pound sausage } Crumble into a large, heavy skillet and cook until pink color disappears. Drain by placing a strainer over a bowl and placing the sausage in the strainer. Let sit until the grease has dripped into the bowl.

1 cup frozen hash browns } Set the unopened package out of the freezer to thaw.

5 eggs, beaten
1/4 cup milk
1 1/2 cups grated cheddar cheese } In a medium bowl, mix together well.

1 package Crescent rolls } Flatten in a 9" x 13" x 2" glass casserole dish. Press edges together to form one solid sheet of dough.

3 TBSP grated parmesan cheese

Spread the thawed hash browns over the crescent roll dough. Top with sausage. Pour egg mixture over the top and sprinkle with parmesan cheese.
Bake in a pre-heated 350⁰ oven for 25 to 30 minutes or until egg mixture is set.
Remove from oven and let cool a few minutes. Cut into squares. Serve with Salsa.

Can't Boil Water #3: To test if an egg dish is "set," insert a case knife (this is a stainless table knife) somewhere close to the center of the dish. If it is not sticky when it is removed, the dish should be done.

BRUNCH HUEVOS RANCHEROS

Cooking spray
4 (6 inch) corn tortillas

Heat a heavy skillet on medium high. Very lightly spray both sides of each tortilla and stack on a paper plate. Cook, one at a time, until they begin to bubble. Turn and repeat on other side. Do not let them get crisp. Remove from skillet and place on a doubled paper towel. Cover with another paper towel to keep warm.

1 cup refried beans with green chilies
2 tsp. butter

Combine in a glass microwave safe dish, cover and cook about 2 minutes or until heated through.

8 slices bacon

Cook in microwave (follow instructions on page 9) until crisp. Crumble into a small bowl and set aside.

4 eggs
2 TBSP butter

Melt butter in the heavy skillet that was used for the corn tortillas, on medium heat. Cook eggs in the butter, fried or scrambled - your choice.

1 cup grated Mexican Blend cheese
1/2 cup Salsa, optional

Place tortillas onto plates. Spread a layer of beans on them. Top with an egg. Divide crumbled bacon onto each tortilla and sprinkle liberally with cheese. Roll them loosely and place on serving plate. Have the Salsa available for those who desire to use it.

BUFFET EGGS

3 TBSP butter
1/3 cup finely chopped green
     onions, including
     the tops
} Melt butter in large heavy skillet. Add onions and tops and cook until tender.

9 eggs
1 1/2 cups dried beef, cut into
     strips
1 cup cottage cheese
} In a medium bowl, beat eggs with a whisk. Using a large spoon, blend in dried beef and cottage cheese.

In a large, heavy skillet, add egg mixture to onion mixture. Stir constantly on medium heat until eggs are scrambled.

Can't Boil Water #4: Always cook eggs on medium temperature. If you cook them on a high temperature, they will be rubbery.

CHRISTMAS BRUNCH CASSEROLE

1 pound sausage
} Crumble sausage into a large skillet and cook over medium heat until evenly browned. Drain by placing a strainer over a bowl and placing the sausage in the strainer until the grease has dripped into the bowl.

6 slices bread, toasted and cut into
     cubes
1/2 pound cheese, grated
1 tsp. dry mustard powder
1/2 tsp. salt
4 eggs, beaten
2 cups milk
} Mix all this together in a large bowl. Add sausage and mix well.

Pour into a greased 9" x 13" x 2" baking dish. Cover and chill in the refrigerator 8 hours or overnight.
Preheat oven to 350^0.
Cover with heavy foil paper and bake for 45 to 60 minutes. Uncover and reduce temperature to 325^0. Bake for an additional 30 minutes or until set.

FRENCH TOAST WAFFLES

Set waffle iron on medium setting.

1 egg, beaten 1/4 cup milk 1/8 tsp. salt 1/4 tsp. vanilla 1 TBSP butter, melted 2 tsp. sugar	Beat all together with a whisk in a medium bowl. Pour into a deep dish pie pan.

4 slices Texas bread or any bread that is sliced about 1" thick.

Dip one slice of bread into the mixture, turning and coating both sides. Bake the coated bread in the hot waffle iron until golden brown (about 2 minutes). Continue until all slices are cooked.
Serve with syrup, marmalade or sift powder sugar over top of waffle.

MOLASSES BREAKFAST BAR

Preheat oven to 350⁰

1 cup butter 1/2 cup dark molasses 1/2 cup brown sugar, packed firmly into cup 4 eggs, beaten	In a large mixing bowl, cream butter until fluffy (Can't Boil Water #7) using an electric hand mixer. Beat in molasses and brown sugar. Stir in eggs using a large spoon.
2 cups flour 1 cup wheat germ 2 tsp. baking powder 1/2 tsp. salt 1 cup regular oats 1 cup raisins 1 cup coarsely chopped walnuts	In a medium bowl, stir all together mixing well. Add to first mixture and stir well.

Grease or spray with cooking spray a jelly roll pan. Spread mixture evenly in pan.
Bake 30 minutes.
Cool in pan, then cut into 1" x 2" bars. Store in ziploc bags.

Can't Boil Water #5: When using brown sugar, always pack it into the measuring cup with the back of a spoon.

OMELET IN A BAG

1 quart size ziploc freezer bag for each person being served

Have each person write their name on a bag with a <u>sharpie permanent marker.</u>
NOTE: Do not use marks-a-lot, it bleeds through the plastic.

2 large or extra large eggs for each bag
NOTE: More eggs per bag will not work

Crack two eggs into a one cup measuring cup, then pour the eggs into a ziploc bag. Seal closed and shake to combine eggs in each bag.

Variety of grated cheeses
Ham pieces
Bacon, cooked drained & crumbled
Onion, chopped
Green pepper, chopped
Tomato, chopped
Pre-cooked hash browns
Salsa

Have each person add ingredients of their choice to their bag. Shake to combine mixture then squeeze out as much air as possible from the bag and zip it up.

Fill a large pot about 2/3 full with water and bring to a boil. Place the bags into boiling water for exactly 13 minutes. 6 to 8 omelets can usually be cooked in one large pot. For more, make another pot of boiling water.

Remove bags, then carefully open each one and slip omelet onto a plate. The omelet will roll out easily.

Be prepared for everyone to be amazed.

NOTE: Great with fresh fruit, coffee cake, or try the Baked French Toast (page 8) in this section of the recipe book.

OATMEAL SUPREME

3/4 cup water
3/4 cup apple cider
1 cup regular oats
1/2 tsp. salt

Bring water and apple cider to a boil in a large, heavy saucepan. Stir in oats and salt. Reduce heat to low and cook 3 minutes, stirring occasionally.

1/2 cup diced pears
1/4 cup sweetened dried cranberries
1/2 tsp. ground cinnamon
1/4 tsp. vanilla extract

Add pears, cranberries, cinnamon and vanilla to oats. Stir gently to combine. Cook 3 minutes or until oats are tender. Remove from stove.

1/4 cup chopped pecans, toasted
1/4 cup milk

Stir into mixture.

Pour into individual serving bowls and serve immediately.

Can't Boil Water #6: Toast pecans ahead of time by spreading them out on a small baking sheet and placing in a 325⁰ oven for 10 minutes. Stir several times during the toasting process to keep them from getting too brown on the bottom. Or, you can follow instructions in Can't Boil Water #25.

PANCAKES

Preheat griddle to 375⁰ or heavy iron skillet on medium-high.

3 eggs 1 tsp. salt 1/4 cup sugar	In a medium bowl mix together, beating well with a whisk.
2 cups milk	Measure into a small bowl and set aside.
2 1/4 cups flour 2 heaping TBSP baking powder	Sift together into a medium bowl.
2 TBSP butter	Melt according to directions Can't Boil Water #2 - page 6, then let cool to warm.

Alternately add milk and flour mixture to egg mixture beating well after each addition. At this point, if the batter is too stiff, add about 1/2 cup Half & Half. Stir well. Add melted butter and stir well.
Pour about 1/4 cup batter onto griddle for each pancake and spread with the bottom of the measuring cup if necessary. Cook until brown then turn and brown on the second side. If not serving immediately, stack on a small plate and keep covered with a tea towel.

SURPRISE POACHED EGGS

This dish is good served with sausages.

2 TBSP butter	Melt in a large skillet.
1 (10 1/2 ounce) can cream of mushroom soup 1 cup milk	Blend together in a medium bowl, using a whisk.

6 to 8 eggs
English Muffins, split and toasted

Add soup mixture to the skillet and heat to boiling. Reduce heat to low. Crack one egg at a time into a 1/2 cup measuring cup and gently slip the egg into the mixture. Repeat until all eggs are slipped into the soup mixture. Cook until egg whites are set (the whites look white and solid).
Place eggs on English muffins and top with sauce from the skillet.

APPETIZERS

&

BEVERAGES

COOKING TERMS

(just a few to get started)

Chop: To cut into irregular pieces.

Cream: To beat shortening, butter or margarine, with or without sugar, until light and fluffy. This process traps in air bubbles, later used to create height in cookies and cakes.

De-glaze: To add liquid to a pan in which foods have been fried or roasted, in order to dissolve the caramelized juices stuck to the bottom of the pan.

Dice: To cut into cubes.

Dot: To sprinkle food with small bits of an ingredient such as butter to allow for even melting.

Drizzle: To pour a liquid such as a sweet glaze or melted butter in a slow, light trickle over food.

Flute: To create a decorative scalloped or rolled edge on a pie crust or other pastry.

Fold: To mix lightly with a spoon to keep as much air in the mixture as possible.

Grind: To cut food into small pieces using a food processor. To grind coarsely, pulse the food processor just a few times until desired size forms.

Juice: Cut orange, lemon or lime in half. Extract juice using a hand or electric juicer. Discard rind.

Knead: To work dough with the heels of the palm of your hands in a pressing and folding motion until it becomes smooth and elastic.

Reserve: To set apart for later use.

Sauté: To cook food quickly in a small amount of fat or oil, until brown, in a skillet over direct heat. The pan and fat must be hot before the food is added; otherwise the food will absorb oil and become soggy.

Separate eggs: Crack an egg. Hold it over a cup and carefully break it apart. Keeping the yolk (yellow part) in one of the shell halves, let the white of the egg (clear in color) slide out and into the cup. Place the yolk into a small bowl and the white into a second small bowl. Repeat as necessary, placing the number of egg yolks and whites needed in the recipe in the separate small bowls.

APPETIZERS

BAKED BRIE WITH RAISIN SAUCE

1 cup raisins 1/4 cup orange liqueur	Microwave liqueur on high for one minute in a small size glass bowl. Add raisins and let stand five minutes.
2 (8 ounce) Brie rounds	Trim rind from the top of Brie rounds, leaving a 1/2" border on each top. Using two 9" pie plates, place one Brie round in each.

3 TBSP honey
Apple & pear slices, peeled or un-peeled, your choice
Assorted crackers

Spoon raisin mixture evenly on Brie rounds. Drizzle evenly with honey.
Bake at 350⁰ for 12 to 15 minutes or until cheese in melted.

This dish can be cooked ahead, covered with nonstick aluminum foil until ready to serve.
Just before serving, cut fruit into medium bowl and toss with a combination of 1 TBSP lemon juice and 1 TBSP water to prevent it from turning brown.
Arrange fruit around Brie on a large serving plate and serve with crackers.

BASIC SOUR CREAM DIP

2 cups (1 pint) sour cream
1 cup cottage cheese
1 TBSP white wine vinegar
    (found on the
    vinegar isle in
    grocery store)
1/2 tsp. celery salt
1/2 tsp onion powder

In a small bowl, mash cottage cheese or press through a small strainer.
Mix all ingredients thoroughly together.

This can be served with crackers or chips.

One of the following can be added for variety.

1 cup shredded crab meat
1 avocado, mashed
2 (3 ounce) cans deviled ham
1 pkg. dry onion or vegetable soup mix
1/2 cup finely minced chives
1 can drained minced clams
1/4 pkg. Taco Seasoning mix

BISCUIT MIX SAUSAGE BALLS

Preheat oven to 350⁰

2 1/2 cups biscuit mix
10 ounces sharp cheddar cheese
16 ounces mild sausage

Measure biscuit mix into a medium size bowl. Grate cheese and crumble sausage over dry mix and combine well.

Roll into balls about the size of a quarter.

Place on a cookie sheet and bake for 15 to 20 minutes.

Do not over bake or they will be dry.
Serve with Basic Sour Cream Dip.

CARAMEL POPCORN CRUNCH

12 cups popped popcorn
1 (3 ounce) can chow
      mein noodles
1 cup dry-roasted peanuts
1/2 cup raisins

Lightly grease a large roasting pan. Combine ingredients in the pan and mix with a large spoon. Set aside.

1 1/2 cups firmly packed
      brown sugar
3/4 cup butter
3/4 cup light corn syrup
1 tsp. ground cinnamon
1/2 tsp. soda

Combine first four ingredients in a heavy, large saucepan. Cook over medium heat, stirring constantly, 5 minutes or until mixture boils. Remove from heat and stir in soda. (Mixture will bubble).

Pour hot mixture over ingredients in the roasting pan and stir.
Bake at 250^0 for 1 hour, stirring every 15 minutes.
Remove from oven and immediately pour onto waxed paper. Break apart large clumps as the mixture cools.
Store in airtight containers.

CHEESE & OLIVE TEA SANDWICHES

1 (4.25 ounce) can chopped ripe
      black olives
1 (4 ounce) package goat cheese
1 green onion, cleaned &
      finely chopped
1 small garlic clove, minced
1/4 tsp. Tabasco sauce

Let cheese soften at room temperature before combining all ingredients in a medium bowl. Stir well.

48 slices Party Bread (miniature
      pkgs. of Rye or
      Pumpernickel bread)

Cut rounds out of each slice using a biscuit cutter that fits the bread.

1/4 cup fresh chopped parsley

The cheese mixture can be prepared up to one day ahead, stored in a covered dish in the refrigerator.

When ready to assemble the sandwiches, spread cheese mixture evenly on half the rounds. Top with remaining rounds.
Roll sides of sandwich in chopped parsley.
Cover and chill for about 2 hours before serving.

CHEESE APPETIZER COOKIES

2 sticks margarine 1 (8 ounce) carton Old English cheese 1/2 tsp. paprika 1/2 tsp. salt	In a medium bowl, cream together well.
2 1/2 cups sifted flour 3/4 cup chopped pecans	Add to first mixture and blend well. It will be a dough like consistency.

Divide dough into four or five pieces and roll into a log shape about 2" diameter. Freeze until very firm.

To prepare, slice thin and bake in a 350⁰ oven for 10 to 12 minutes.

To prepare, slice thin and bake in a 350^0 oven for 10 to 12 minutes.

Can't Boil Water #7: Old English cheese usually comes in a small glass jar and is found in the cheese section. It is a soft, smoky type cheese.

CHEESE BALL

2 (3 ounce) wedges Roquefort
      cheese
2 (5 ounce) jars processed cheddar
      cheese spread
2 TBSP minced onion
1 tsp. Worcestershire sauce
1/2 cup snipped parsley
1 cup ground pecans (do this in
      the blender or food
      processor)
	Reserve half the parsley and pecans for later use.
	Combine remainder of ingredients in a medium bowl using an electric mixer.

Form into two balls. Wrap in plastic wrap and refrigerate overnight.

Just before serving, unwrap cheese balls and roll in the remaining parsley and pecans.

Serve with chips or favorite crackers.

CHEESE DAINTIES

1 egg white (check page 18 to separate egg) } In a medium bowl, slightly beat the egg white with a small whisk. Set aside.

1/2 cup butter, softened
1 cup grated sharp cheddar cheese
1 1/2 cups sifted flour
1 TBSP Worcestershire sauce
1/4 tsp. Cayenne pepper
1/4 tsp. paprika
1 tsp. salt
} Mix together using an electric hand mixer until well blended. Shape into small balls.

50 pecan halves

Place balls on ungreased cookie sheet. Press with a fork.
Brush bottom of each pecan half with egg white and press onto top of each cookie.
Bake in a 325^0 oven for 25 minutes.

CHEESE-NUT BALL

1/4 pound blue cheese
1/4 pound cheddar cheese spread
3 ounce cream cheese
} Soften cheeses to room temperature in a medium bowl, then using an electric mixer at low speed, mix together very well.

1 medium onion, grated
1 tsp. steak sauce
1 1/2 cups chopped pecans, divided
} Add onion, steak sauce and half the pecans to the cheese mixture. Mix well with a spoon.

2 TBSP chopped parsley } Keep in the refrigerator, in a small jar with a lid. Be sure to tighten the lid on the jar to keep the parsley fresh. Will be used the next day.

Refrigerate mixture, covered with plastic wrap, 1 hour. Shape into a large ball.
Wrap in waxed paper and refrigerate overnight.
One hour before serving, remove and roll in remaining pecans then parsley.
Place on serving dish and cover lightly until ready to serve.
Arrange crackers or party bread around the ball.

CHILI CHEESE LOG

1 pkg. dry chili seasoning
2 (8 ounce) pkgs. cream cheese
3 TBSP salsa

} Soften cream cheese in a medium bowl and add seasoning mix, then salsa. Mix well
Shape into a log.

1 cup chopped pecans
1 cup Monterey Jack cheese

} Roll log in pecans, then cheese.

Wrap in plastic wrap and refrigerate until ready to serve.

Can't Boil Water #8: Spray hands with cooking spray to keep mixture from sticking while molding a cheese log into shape.

CHUTNEY CHEESE SPREAD

2 (3 ounce) pkgs. cream cheese
1 cup grated sharp cheese
2 TBSP dry sherry
1/2 tsp. curry powder
1/4 tsp. salt

} In a medium bowl, soften cream cheese and combine with remaining ingredients. Blend well.

1/4 cup finely chopped chutney
1 TBSP finely snipped chives

} Reserve chives. Stir chutney into mixture.

Place mixture into a serving dish and top with the chives.

Can't Boil Water #9: Green onion tops can be substituted for the chives.

CUCUMBER SANDWICH SPREAD

1 small cucumber 3 green onions	} Chop cucumber very fine. Chop onions, including tops.
2 (8 ounce) pkgs. cream cheese 1/2 tsp. garlic salt Dash of dill weed 1 TBSP salad dressing 1 TBSP lemon juice	} Combine in a medium bowl, mixing well.

Add cucumber and onion to cream cheese mixture blending well. Chill, covered, overnight.

Can't Boil Water #10: When boiling eggs. Place eggs in a heavy saucepan that is large enough to hold eggs in a single layer. Cover eggs with water, sprinkle salt on top of each egg. Bring water to a boil. Boil 1 minute. Cover pan, remove from heat and let set 20 minutes. Drain and add some ice, then cover with cold water to cool the eggs. Crack eggs all around and peel under running water.

CURRIED EGG SANDWICHES

3 hard-cooked eggs 1/4 cup mayonnaise 1 1/2 tsp. curry powder 3 TBSP chopped ripe olives Dash salt	} Place in a food processor and, using the stainless blade, pulse 6 to 8 times or until eggs are finely chopped.
10 slices of thin sliced bread Soft butter Sliced ripe olives	} Spread butter on one side of each bread slice. Spread egg mixture on top.

Cut each bread slice into four pieces. Garnish with olive slices.

NOTE: The egg mixture may be refrigerated, covered, overnight.
    If you prefer, you can mash eggs very fine with the back of the tines of a fork, then add remaining ingredients.

DILL DIP

1 (3 ounce) pkg. cream cheese
1 TBSP finely chopped stuffed
        green olives
1 tsp. grated onion
1/4 tsp. dried dill weed
Dash salt
2 TBSP cream or half & half

In a medium bowl, soften cheese and add the next four ingredients. Stir in cream one TBSP at a time until the mixture is of dipping consistency. It may not be necessary to use all the cream.

Chill, covered, until ready to serve.
Zucchini, celery sticks or cauliflower broken into small pieces are good served with this dip.

EGG SALAD SANDWICH FILLING

1 dozen hard boiled eggs
4 green onions, cut into
        small pieces
1/4 cup coarsely chopped
        fresh chives
1/4 cup mayonnaise
1 TBSP Dijon mustard
1 tsp. seasoned salt
Pepper to taste

Place in a food processor and, using the stainless blade, pulse 6 to 8 times or until eggs are finely chopped.

Remove mixture from the food processor and place into a covered container.
Store in refrigerator until ready to make sandwiches.
Can be stored about 2 days.

Can't Boil Water #11: To keep filling from making the bread soggy, spread a thin layer of soft butter over the bread first.

FRUIT DIP

1 pint marshmallow cream
8 ounces cream cheese

} In a medium bowl, let cream cheese soften to room temperature, then add marshmallow cream and mix together well.

2 TBSP milk
Cinnamon

} Add to cream cheese mixture and mix well.

1 TBSP orange zest or orange juice can be added instead of the cinnamon. Refrigerate, covered, until ready to serve.

GARLIC CHEESE BALL

8 ounces cream cheese
8 ounces cracker barrel
        sharp cheese
1 clove garlic, minced
1/2 cup chopped pecans

} Soften cream cheese in a medium bowl, then grate sharp cheese over the top. Mix together using an electric mixer until well blended. Add garlic and pecans mixing well with a spoon.

Chili powder

Shape mixture into a ball and sprinkle with chili powder. Place on a cheese plate, cover and refrigerate until ready to serve.

GRAPE WIENIES

1 to 2 pounds Little Smokes (or
         similar brand)
1 small jar grape jelly
1 medium bottle ketchup

Cut sausages into small pieces. Combine all ingredients in a crock pot.

Cook 4 hours on low or 2 hours on high.

This recipe will work well with sugar free jelly, low calorie ketchup and turkey wienies.

HAM & DEVILS

6 hard-cooked eggs
3 TBSP minced ham
2 TBSP mayonnaise
2 TBSP softened cream cheese
1 tsp. mustard
1 tsp. lemon or pickle juice
1/2 tsp. dill weed
1/2 tsp. caraway seeds

Cut eggs in half lengthwise, place yolks in a small bowl and set egg whites aside. Mash yolks, then mix in remaining ingredients except egg whites.

Fill egg whites with mixture. Cover and refrigerate until ready to serve.

LATIN DEVILS

6 hard-cooked eggs
2 TBSP undrained canned
    chopped green chilies
2 TBSP canned corn kernels
2 TBSP minced green onions
    with tops
2 TBSP grated Jack cheese
2 TBSP taco sauce

Cut eggs in half lengthwise, place yolks in a small bowl and set egg whites aside. Mash yolks, then mix in remaining ingredients except egg whites.

Fill egg whites and store, covered, in the refrigerator until ready to serve.

LAYERED MEXICAN DIP

1 large can refried beans
1 pkg. dry taco seasoning mix

Mix together in a small bowl, using 1/2 to 1 pkg. taco seasoning, according to your taste.
Spread on a pizza pan leaving room around the edge of the pan to layer chips.

1 small carton sour cream
1 small container guacamole dip
1 small can chopped green chilies
1 small can chopped black olives,
    drained
1 large tomato, chopped
1 small pkg. grated cheese
Nacho chips

Spread remaining ingredients on top of bean mixture following order given. Place nacho chips around edge of the pan.

Cover and refrigerate until ready to serve.

MEXICAN FUDGE

1 pound grated cheese } Spread half the cheese in a 9"x 11" baking dish.

3 eggs, beaten well
1/2 cup green salsa } Combine and spread on the cheese layer.

Spread remaining cheese on top.
Bake in a 350⁰ oven for 30 minutes.
Cool 10 minutes and cut into 1" squares.

OYSTER CRACKERS

1 package dry Ranch House
        Dressing Mix
1 cup cooking oil
1 tsp. dill weed
1 tsp. lemon pepper
1/4 tsp. cayenne pepper
1/2 tsp. Salad Seasoning } Combine in an extra large glass mixing bowl. Cover with waxed paper and microwave on high 3 minutes. Stir well.

2 (10 ounce) pkgs. oyster crackers } Add crackers to mixture and stir well with a large spoon until well coated.

Store in ziploc bags.
Serve as a snack or with soups or stews.

PIMENTO CHEESE

1 (16 slices) pkg. American cheese
1 (2 ounce) jar chopped pimentos
1 (5 ounce) can canned milk
3/4 to 1 cup salad dressing such
        as Miracle Whip or
        Hellmann's

In top of a double boiler, over the bottom pan of water, melt cheese. As it melts, slowly begin adding milk, stirring until well blended. Add pimentos. Remove top pan from heat and add 3/4 cup salad dressing. Stir well. If the mixture is too thin, add remaining salad dressing.

The mixture will be kind of thin but not runny. Cool completely before storing in refrigerator, tightly covered. It will have a better spreading texture after refrigerating several hours.
Serve as a dip or can be used to make a sandwich.

POPCORN SCRAMBLE

6 cups popcorn, popped
2 cups cheerios
2 cups rice chex
1 cup nuts

Place in a large roasting pan and mix together.

1 stick butter
1 cup brown sugar
1/4 cup karo syrup
1/4 tsp. baking soda
1 tsp. vanilla

Heat butter, brown sugar, syrup in a small saucepan until it begins to boil. Remove from heat and add baking soda and vanilla. Stir well.

Pour liquid mixture over the dry ingredients and mix together well.
Bake in a 250⁰ oven for 1 hour. Stir half way through cooking time.
Store in an air-tight container. Ziplocs are great for this type storage.

"PUPPY CHOW"

3/4 cups shelled sunflower kernels
1 pkg. chocolate chips or peanut
            butter chips
1 cup raisins
3/4 cup peanuts or pecans   } Mix well in a large bowl.
2 cups crunchy cereal
        (Like Crunchy Oat Bran)
1 cup dried cranberries or craisins

Divide into small baggies.

This is a great recipe for Halloween or brown bagging.

RED DEVIL BALLS

1 (4.50 ounce) can deviled ham
1 (8 ounce) pkg. cream cheese

Cut cream cheese into cubes and put into blender container along with the ham. Cover and process until smooth, using a rubber spatula, taking care not to get it in the blades, to aid processing.

1 cup pecans, chopped very fine

Remove mixture from blender container to a small container, cover and chill in the refrigerator until firm enough to shape into small balls. Roll each ball in pecans. Serve on wooden picks.

SALMON SPREAD

1 large can salmon, drained &
    de-boned
2 (8 ounce) pkgs. cream cheese
3 TBSP lemon juice
3 TBSP milk
1 1/2 tsp. dill weed
1/4 cup finely chopped onion
3 to 4 drops liquid smoke

In a medium bowl, soften cream cheese using a fork or the back of a spoon. Add remaining ingredients and blend well.

Cover, then keep refrigerated until ready to serve.

NOTE: You can omit milk, but may need to add some liquid from the salmon.

SAUSAGE ROLL

1 pkg. hot-spicy sausage

Crumble sausage into a large skillet and cook over medium heat until evenly browned. Drain by placing a strainer over a bowl and placing the sausage in the strainer until the grease has dripped into the bowl. Rinse sausage with hot water and drain again.

1 (8 ounce) pkg. cream cheese

Soften at room temperature, then combine in a medium bowl with the cooked sausage. Mix well.

1 egg white (check page 18 to
    separate eggs)
1 TBSP water

Mix together in a 1 cup measuring cup and set aside.

2 pkgs. Crescent Rolls
Poppy seeds

Open Crescent Rolls and remove 4 triangles intact and press seams together to form a square. there will be 4 squares total. Place 1/4 of the sausage mixture down the center of each square, forming a log, and press the crescent squares together around log of sausage. Repeat for each "log." Flip "logs" over so the seam is on the bottom and brush with the egg white mixture. Sprinkle with poppy seeds.
Place on a cookie sheet and bake in a 375^0 oven for 15 minutes.

SPINACH DIP

1 (10 ounce) pkg. frozen spinach
1 (16 ounce) carton sour cream
1 cup mayonnaise
1 (8 ounce) can sliced water
    chestnuts
3 green onions, chopped
1 pkg. Knorr vegetable soup mix

Thaw and drain spinach well. Drain and chop water chestnuts. Clean onions then chop including about half of the green tops.

In a medium bowl, mix all ingredients together. Cover and chill in the refrigerator at least 2 hours before serving.

Optional: Add 2 cups grated cheese.
           Plain yogurt can be substituted for the sour cream.
Serve with chips or crackers, or trim the top off and hollow out a loaf of round bread, then place the dip inside for a festive look.

SPINACH PIMENTO DIP

14 ounce carton pimento cheese*
1/2 cup sour cream
1 (10 ounce) pkg. frozen spinach
3 TBSP parsley

Thaw, drain well and chop spinach. Place in a medium bowl, then combine with remaining ingredients.

Cover and refrigerate until ready to serve.

*Optional: Use equal amount (about 1 3/4 cups) of homemade pimento cheese.

Great served with Melba toast, chips, crackers, or party bread (page 70 tells you about party bread.)

TUNA PATÉ

2 (8 ounce) pkgs. cream cheese 2 (6.5 ounce) cans tuna in water 3 green onions, include tops 1/2 cup chili sauce 3 dashes hot pepper sauce 1/8 tsp. garlic powder 3 dashes Worcestershire sauce	In a medium bowl, soften cream cheese. Using a strainer, drain tuna and discard the liquid. Clean and chop onions.

Parsley flakes (optional)

Combine all ingredients in the bowl with the cream cheese, mixing well.
Place in a mold, cover and chill overnight.
Remove cover and un-mold onto a serving plate, then garnish with parsley flakes, if desired.

Can't Boil Water #12: Lightly coat inside of mold with cooking spray before placing mixture in it.

TUTI-FRUITI

1 banana, peeled and sliced 1/2 cantaloupe, peeled with seeds removed and cut into small pieces 1/2 pound grapes, wash, remove stems & cut each grape in half 2 kiwifruit, peeled and diced into medium size pieces 1 orange, peeled, sectioned and diced into bite size pieces 12 strawberries, washed & sliced	Mix together in a large bowl.
2 TBSP powdered sugar 1 TBSP lemon juice	Mix together in a small bowl and pour over fruit. Toss together.

Cover and refrigerate until ready to serve.

VEGETABLE DIP

1 can tomato soup
1 (3 ounce) pkg. lemon jello
3 (8 ounce) pkgs. cream cheese
1/2 cup water

Mix tomato soup and jello in a medium saucepan. Dice cream cheese and add to mixture. Add water. Melt mixture over LOW heat stirring often.

1 cup green bell pepper, chopped
    (remove seeds before chopping)
1/2 cup chopped pecans
1/2 cup peeled, chopped onion
1 cup salad dressing

Combine with first mixture until well mixed.

Refrigerate, covered, overnight.
Serve with fresh vegetables or chips.
Makes a large amount.

YUMMY CARAMEL DIP

1 stick butter
1 cup packed brown sugar
8 ounces cream cheese
8 ounces caramel sauce
    (this is an ice cream topping)

Soften butter and cream cheese at room temperature. In a medium bowl, blend well with sugar until creamy. Add caramel sauce and blend well.

Cover and keep refrigerated until ready to serve.
Serve with apple slices or other fruit.

NOTE: To soften butter and/or cream cheese, unwrap and let set on the open wrapper until soft.

BEVERAGES

CRANBERRY PUNCH

1 cup canned cranberry sauce 1 1/2 cups hot water	In a medium bowl, dissolve sauce in the hot water.
1/2 cup concentrated lemon juice (found in frozen juice section in grocery store) 3 1/2 cups sugar 1/2 cup orange juice	Add to first mixture.
2 1/2 cups water 1 TBSP whole cloves 3 to 4 cinnamon sticks	Tie cloves in a gauze bag. Combine with cinnamon sticks and water in a medium saucepan. Boil until the water is very pink.

Remove spices and combine all ingredients.
Serve very warm.

Can't Boil Water #13: Taste test the spice-water mixture to determine if it is strong enough. Keep in mind that it will be diluted somewhat when combined with the other ingredients.

HOLIDAY PUNCH

2 (10 ounce) jars raspberry jelly
2 cups boiling water

> In a large heat proof bowl, using a whisk, beat jelly until smooth. Gradually add boiling water. Continue beating until jelly is dissolved.

1 (6 ounce) can frozen
       orange juice

> Stir into jelly mixture. Chill.

1 pint cranberry juice
6 (7 ounce) bottles lemon-lime
       soda
2 cups ice cubes

> Chill until ready to use.

When ready to serve, pour chilled jelly mixture into a punch bowl. Add cranberry juice. Slowly pour in chilled soda. Add ice cubes. Stir until just blended.

ORANGE JULEP

2 family size or 5 regular size
       tea bags
2 (2 1/2 inch) cinnamon sticks
1 quart boiling water

> Place tea bags and cinnamon sticks in a heat proof pitcher, pour boiling water in pitcher and let tea steep 10 minutes. Remove tea bags and cinnamon sticks.

2 cups cold water
2 1/2 cups orange juice
1 1/2 cups cranberry juice cocktail

> Add cold water to first mixture and stir to cool. Add remaining juices.

Chill until ready to serve.
Serve over crushed ice. Drop a mint leaf on top if desired.

PEACH PUNCH

2 (3 ounce) pkgs. peach jello
2 cups very hot water
2 cups sugar
} In a large bowl, dissolve jello in water, stirring well. Add sugar and stir until dissolved.

2 large cans Hi-C Peach
4 cups water
} Add to jello mixture and stir well. Pour into a large plastic container and freeze to a slush.

2 bottles Ginger Ale

When ready to serve, place slush into a large punch bowl and add Ginger Ale. Stir gently.

NOTE: If Hi-C peach cannot be found, use 1 large bottle of mango peach and 4 (12 ounce) cans peach nectar.

PERCOLATOR PUNCH

3 quarts apple juice
1 quart pineapple juice
1 quart cranberry juice
1 large pkg. red hots
} Pour juices in a large electric coffee percolator, insert stem and basket. Pour red hots into the basket and perk.

Recipe can be reduced for a smaller percolator.

SPICED TEA

3 cups sugar
1 1/2 cups water
} Place in a medium saucepan and bring to a boil. Reduce heat and cook until sugar is dissolved. Let cool.

3 large tea bags
4 quarts boiling water
} Place tea bags in a large heat proof pitcher. Pour in water and let steep about 20 minutes. Remove tea bags.

8 lemons
1 orange
1/2 tsp. cinnamon
1/2 tsp. cloves
} In a small bowl, grate rind of lemons and orange. Set aside. Juice lemons and orange. Combine juice with rind and spices.

Combine all mixtures in the large pitcher or a very large cooking pot. Serve hot or cold. Keep refrigerated.

SPICE TEA MIX
ACK's original sugar free

2 1/2 cups sugar substitute
4 (0.15 ounce) pkgs. no sugar lemon kool-aid
4 (0.15 ounce) pkgs. no sugar orange kool-aid
1 1/2 cup instant decaf tea
1 tsp. cloves
2 tsp. cinnamon
} Combine in a medium bowl.

Store in a quart size glass jar with a tight fitting lid.
Use 2 tsp. of the mix in 1 cup hot water.

TEA SYRUP

1 cup loose tea leaves (regular
      dark tea leaves,
      full strength)
4 cups water

} Combine in a large saucepan and bring to a boil. Reduce heat and cook for about 2 minutes. Remove from heat and let steep for about 20 minutes.

4 cups sugar

Using a large, heat proof jar with a screw on lid, pour sugar into the jar and strain the hot tea liquid over the sugar. Stir until sugar is dissolved.
Store in refrigerator.
Use 2 TBSP tea syrup for each large glass filled with water and ice.

NOTE: Label the jar so no one will use too much of the syrup.

VEGETABLE JUICE COCKTAILS

1 cup juice drained from either
      peas or green beans
2 cups canned tomato juice
3 to 4 sprigs celery leaves
1/2 tsp. salt
Dash pepper
1/8 tsp. minced onion
2 tsp. lemon juice
2 drops Worcestershire sauce

} In a one quart pitcher, mix juices, then add celery leaves. Cover tightly and chill for 1 hour.
Remove celery leaves and add remaining ingredients.

Refrigerate until very cold.

WATERMELON COOLER

6 cups chopped watermelon
1/4 cup raspberries
1 cup water
1/4 cup sugar
1/2 cup lemon juice

Remove seeds from watermelon and use only the red part of the melon. Blend watermelon with raspberries in a blender, using the stainless blade, until smooth. Strain through a fine strainer into a 2 quart pitcher. Discard what is left in the strainer. Stir in sugar and lemon juice until sugar dissolves.

Cover and refrigerate until chilled.

SALADS
&
SOUPS

SALAD TIPS

Do not use metal bowls when mixing salads. Use wood, glass or china.

If the ingredients of a salad recipe has garlic listed, then before mixing the salad in a wooden bowl, take one clove of the garlic and cut it in half, then rub it all around the inside of the bowl. This will enhance the flavor of the salad.

If using bananas in a salad, then be sure to add them just before serving to keep them fresh.

SALADS

APRICOT-NUT CHICKEN SALAD

1 1/2 cups shredded cooked
               chicken breast
1/2 cup thinly sliced celery
1/4 cup mayonnaise
2 TBSP chopped, unsalted
           cashews
2 TBSP chopped dried apricots
2 TBSP chopped green onions
2 TBSP plain yogurt
1/2 tsp. salt
1/8 tsp. black pepper

To shred the chicken, tear it into thin strips then measure the 1 1/2 cups. Combine all ingredients in a large bowl and mix well.

Refrigerate, covered, until ready to serve.
Can be served as a salad or in a sandwich.

ARGYLE SALAD

1 cup fruit juice (pineapple or
            orange)
Juice of 1 lemon
1 large can fruit cocktail

Drain fruit cocktail juice into a medium saucepan. Reserve the fruit for later use. Add remaining juices and heat on medium. Do not boil.

1 egg, beaten
1/4 cup flour
2 TBSP sugar
Dash salt
10 large marshmallows

In a medium bowl, beat together egg, flour, sugar and salt, then add to the fruit juices in the saucepan. Cook at medium temperature until thick. Remove from heat and add marshmallows. Stir well. Pour into a medium bowl, cover and chill.

1 cup pecans
1 cup maraschino cherries, drained
1 can black binge cherries, drained
2 bananas, cut into chunks
1 cup heavy cream, whipped

Before serving, add pecans, both cherries and bananas. Stir well. Fold in whipped cream.

45

BAKED FRUIT MEDLEY

1 orange
1 lemon

> Grate rind of each fruit into a small bowl and set aside. Peel each fruit and slice. Layer the slices in a 9" x 13" x 2" glass baking dish.

1 (16 ounce) can sliced peaches
1 (16 ounce) can pear halves
1 (16 ounce) can apricots
1 (15.25 ounce) can sliced pineapple
1 (6 ounce) jar maraschino cherries

> Drain all fruits well and layer over the orange and lemon slices. (Reserve the juice from the fruits and store in a large jar with a lid in the refrigerator. The combination makes an excellent breakfast drink.)

1 cup firmly packed brown sugar
1 TBSP flour
1 TBSP Angostura bitters (can be found in the grocery store)

> Combine grated rind, brown sugar, flour and bitters. Mix well. Sprinkle over fruit.

Bake in a 325⁰ oven for 30 minutes or until bubbly.
Can be served hot or chilled.

CABBAGE SALAD

1 head cabbage, chopped
1 onion, cleaned & diced
1 green pepper, seeds removed & diced

> Combine in a large bowl and mix well.

1/4 cup pimento
1/2 cup vinegar
1/2 cup salad oil
1/2 cup sugar
1 tsp. salt
1 1/2 TBSP prepared mustard
1 TBSP celery seed

> Mix together in a medium size saucepan and bring to a boil. Pour over cabbage mixture and mix well.

Put into a dish that has a tight lid and refrigerate over night.
This stays good for a week refrigerated.

Can't Boil Water #14: Salad oil and cooking oil are basically the same. Just depends on how the recipe reads. Peanut oil is basically used in oriental dishes. Olive oil should be extra virgin, light.

CHERRY COKE SALAD

1 (12 ounce) can Coca Cola
1 (15 ounce) can black pitted
    cherries
1 (20 ounce) can crushed
    pineapple
2 (3 ounce) boxes cherry jello

} Drain cherries and pineapple, reserving juice. Set aside fruit. In a medium saucepan, combine coke and juice from both fruits. Bring to a boil. Remove from heat and add jello, stirring until dissolved. Let cool somewhat.

1 cup chopped pecans

} Add pecans, cherries and pineapple to the cooled mixture.

Pour into a medium sized glass pan and refrigerate several hours or overnight. Serve individual squares on a lettuce leaf and top with salad dressing such as Miracle Whip.

If serving as a dessert, top with whipped cream or whipped topping.

CHICKEN SALAD

4 cups diced cooked chicken
1 1/2 cups diced celery

} Combine in a large bowl.

1 cup mayonnaise
2 TBSP lemon juice
1 tsp. salt
1/8 tsp. pepper

} Blend together in a small bowl, then toss lightly with the chicken-celery mixture. Cover and refrigerate until chilled.

Salad greens, your choice

Serve on the salad greens. Garnish with additional mayonnaise, if desired.

Add whole green grapes and walnuts chopped medium for a different salad.

NOTE: Canned chicken, drained, can be used. It is found next to canned tuna in the grocery store.

COOKIE SALAD

1 (3.5 ounce) pkg. instant vanilla
         pudding
1/2 cup buttermilk

} In a large bowl, mix together well.

1 (20 ounce) can crushed
         pineapple
1 (11 ounce) can mandarin
         oranges
1 (16 ounce) tub whipped topping
1 pkg. pecan sandies cookies

} Drain fruits well. Break cookies into small pieces. Add everything to the pudding mixture, stirring well.

Refrigerate, covered, until well chilled before serving.

CRANBERRY FLUFF

1 pound fresh cranberries
1 (11 ounce) can mandarin
         oranges
1 (20 ounce) can crushed
         pineapple
1 Delicious apple
1 cup chopped pecans
2 cups miniature marshmallows
1 cup sugar

} Coarsely grind cranberries in a blender. Drain oranges and pineapple very well. Core and coarsely dice apple. In a large bowl, mix all ingredients well. Cover and chill in refrigerator overnight.

1 (12 ounce) carton whipped topping

Drain mixture well and add whipped topping.
This makes a beautiful pie filling in a baked graham cracker crust.
If you want to use this recipe for a relish, omit the whipped topping.

CRANBERRY SALAD

1 1/2 cups boiling water 1 cup sugar 1 (3 ounce) pkg. cherry jello 1 (3 ounce) pkg. lemon jello	In a large bowl, dissolve jello's and sugar in the boiling water.
1 TBSP lemon juice 1 cup raw cranberries, ground 1 whole orange, ground 1 cup chopped celery 1/2 cup chopped nuts 1 (20 ounce) can crushed pineapple, including juice	Remove seeds from orange before grinding. Add all ingredients to jello mixture and pour into a mold. Remember to spray mold lightly with cooking spray. Refrigerate until set.

Before serving, un-mold onto a serving plate. Arrange lettuce leaves around the salad.

CREAMY CHERRY JELLO SALAD

1 (15 ounce) can cherry pie filling 1 (20 ounce) can crushed pineapple 1/2 cup sugar 1 cup miniature marshmallows	Drain pineapple well. Mix all ingredients in a medium bowl and refrigerate, covered, over night.
1/2 cup chopped pecans 1 (12 ounce) carton whipped topping 2 bananas, sliced (optional)	Next day, add ingredients to previous mixture. Stir until blended.

EGG SALAD

1/4 cup mayonnaise
1 TBSP chopped fresh dill
1 TBSP grated onion
1 TBSP dill pickle relish   Stir together in a large bowl.
1 TBSP prepared mustard
1/4 tsp. pepper
1/8 tsp. salt

8 hard-cooked eggs, peeled and coarsely chopped

Gently stir eggs into mixture.
Cover and chill in refrigerator at least 2 hours or up to 2 days.
Serve on small party bread or crackers.

FRITO SALAD

1" thick Longhorn round cheese
6 slices bacon, fried very crisp,
         then crumbled
1 bunch green onions with tops,   Using 3/4 of the cheese, grate it
       cleaned & chopped   into a medium bowl, then mix in
2 hard-cooked eggs,   bacon, onions, eggs and tomato.
       peeled & chopped   Add dressing to taste.
1 tomato, chopped
Wishbone Red Russian Dressing

1 (4.5 ounce) pkg. corn chips, crushed

Refrigerate until ready to serve.
Just before serving, add corn chips.

NOTE: If cheese has a red rind around it, be sure to remove and discard
the rind before using the cheese. Store unused portion in a ziploc bag in the
refrigerator.

FROZEN CRANBERRY SALAD

1 (8 ounce) pkg. cream cheese
1/2 cup sugar
1 (16 ounce) can whole-berry
        cranberry sauce

} In a large bowl, beat cream cheese and sugar until creamy. Add cranberry sauce and mix well.

1 (20 ounce) can crushed
        pineapple, drained
1/2 cup chopped pecans
1 (12 ounce) carton whipped
        topping
2 peeled, mashed bananas
        (optional)

} Fold into the cheese cranberry mixture according to order given. Stir well.

Spoon into a 9" x 13" x 2" glass dish. Cover tightly and freeze.
To serve, cut into squares and, if desired, place each square on a lettuce leaf.

FROZEN FRUIT SALAD

1 quart frozen whipped topping
1 pint sour cream
1 1/2 cup sugar

} Mix together in a large bowl well.

1 cup chopped pecans
4 TBSP lemon juice
1 (20 ounce) can crushed
        pineapple drained
5 large bananas, mashed
1 cup maraschino cherries,
        chopped

} Stir well into first mixture.

Pour into two 7 1/4" x 12" glass dishes. Cover tightly and freeze.
When ready to serve, cut into squares.
May be used as a salad or dessert.

FROZEN YOGURT SALAD

2 (8 ounce) cartons fruit yogurt
1/2 cup sugar   } In a large bowl, blend until smooth.
1/4 cup mayonnaise

1 (11 ounce) can mandarin
        oranges, drained
1 (1 pound 10 ounce) can fruit
        cocktail, drained   } Stir fruit into yogurt mixture.
1 large banana, sliced
1 large apple, peeled, cored &
        chopped

12 Maraschino cherries with stems

Spoon mixture, divided evenly, into each cup of a 12 cup muffin pan lined with
paper baking cups. Top with cherries. Freeze at least 6 hours. When ready to
serve, remove from paper cups and place in individual serving dishes.

FRUIT SALAD DRESSING

1 cup salad dressing (such as
        Miracle Whip or   Mix salad dressing and honey in a
        Hellmann's)   } small bowl until smooth. Gradually
3/4 cup honey   add oil, stirring after each addition.
1/3 cup salad oil   Add poppy seed.
1 tsp. poppy seed

Store in a jar with a screw-on lid in the refrigerator until ready to use.
Using any type fruit, place in a individual serving dish and drizzle 1 to 2 TBSP
of the salad dressing on top.

GRAPE SALAD

1 (8 ounce) pkg. cream cheese
3 TBSP sour cream
1 (7 ounce) jar marshmallow
    cream
} In a large bowl, cream together well.

1 to 1 1/2 pounds red and/or
    green grapes, whole
1 cup chopped pecans or walnuts
} Wash the grapes and pluck from the stems. Drain well. Add, along with the nuts to the cream cheese mixture and blend well.

Cover and refrigerate.
Best served very chilled.

HOT GERMAN POTATO SALAD

6 baking potatoes
1 pound bacon, chopped
} Wash and scrub potatoes and cook in a large pot, un-peeled, in boiling water until tender when pierced with a fork.
Fry bacon until crisp. Remove bacon from skillet and place on several layers of paper towels to drain. Reserve 2 TBSP bacon grease.

1/3 cup vinegar
2 tsp. salt
1/4 tsp. pepper
3/4 cup cleaned, chopped green
    onion
} Combine in a large bowl.

Peel and slice the potatoes 1/8" thick and place into the vinegar mixture. Add bacon and 2 TBSP reserved bacon grease.
Serve on lettuce with big frankfurters or German sausage.

INDIAN SLAW

1 pkg. cole slaw mix (in produce
    isle in grocery
    store)
2 pkgs. chicken flavor Ramen
    Noodles
1 cup silvered almonds, toasted
1 cup sunflower seeds
6 green onions, cleaned &
    chopped

} Mix together in a large bowl.

DRESSING:

1 cup salad oil
1/3 cup vinegar, white or dark
1/3 cup sugar
2 seasoning packets from Ramen
    Noodles

} Mix well and pour over the salad.

Keep refrigerated until ready to serve.

LIME-SOUR CREAM SALAD

1 (8.25 ounce) can crushed
    pineapple
1 cup water
1 (3 ounce) pkg. lime jello
1 cup sour cream
1 cup green grapes

} Drain pineapple, reserving 1 cup juice in a small bowl. In a medium saucepan, boil water and add juice. Add jello, stirring until jello is dissolved. Pour into a medium bowl and chill.
Fold in sour cream and fruit.
Pour into a 4 cup mold sprayed with cooking spray.
Refrigerate until set.

BANANA CREAM DRESSING

1 banana
1/2 cup sour cream
1/2 cup brown sugar

} Peel then slice banana into a blender container. Add sour cream and brown sugar and blend until smooth.

Un-mold the jello mixture over lettuce leaves that have been arranged on a serving plate. Drizzle dressing over the top.

LUNCHEON SALAD

1 can tomato soup
1 TBSP gelatin, softened in 1/4
    cup water

Heat soup to boiling in a large
saucepan. Remove from heat. Stir
in gelatin until dissolved. Cool.

1 cup mayonnaise
1/2 cup finely chopped celery
1 medium green pepper, chopped
1/4 cup chopped stuffed olives
2 (3 ounce) pkgs. cream cheese,
    softened

Add mayonnaise and cream cheese
to soup mixture and blend until
smooth. Add remaining
ingredients. Stir well.

Spoon into an 8" x 10" mold that has been sprayed with cooking spray.
Refrigerate for several hours or overnight.
Un-mold the congealed salad onto a serving plate.

MY FAVORITE TUNA SALAD

3 (6 ounce) cans tuna in water,
    well drained
3 eggs, hard boiled, peeled and
    chopped
2 ribs celery, chopped
1/4 cup chopped salad olives
1 large red delicious apple, cored,
    peeled and chopped
2 to 3 TBSP sweet pickle relish
2/3 to 3/4 cup salad dressing
Salt and pepper to taste
1/4 cup chopped pecans or
    walnuts

Mix all together, in a large bowl.
Transfer to a smaller container, then
cover and chill.

Very good with Cabbage Patch Bread, page 75.

NOTE: Refer to Can't Boil Water #10 to boil eggs.

OLD FASHIONED COLE SLAW

4 pounds chopped or shredded
        cabbage
1 cup chopped onions

} Put in a very large bowl and set aside.

3/4 cup sugar
3/4 cup vinegar
1/3 cup salad oil
1/2 tsp. pepper
1/4 tsp. salt
1 tsp. dry mustard

} Place ingredients in a medium size sauce pan. Mix together well. Heat to a boil. Remove from heat and set aside.

Pour sugar-vinegar mixture over the cabbage and onions just before serving, mixing well.

PATTON'S FRUIT SALAD

1 (16 ounce) can peach pie filling
1 (20 ounce) can pineapple tidbits,
        drained
1 (11 ounce) can Mandarin
        oranges, drained
1 (12 ounce) pkg. strawberries,
        thawed
1 banana, sliced

} Mix all together in a medium bowl.

Refrigerate, covered, until well chilled.

PISTACHIO SALAD

1 pkg. pistachio instant pudding
1 (12 ounce) can crushed
    pineapple
} Mix together in a medium size bowl.

1 cup miniature marshmallows
1/2 cup chopped pecans
1 (12 ounce) carton whipped
    topping
} Add to first mixture and stir well.

Refrigerate covered, until ready to serve.

RANCH PICNIC POTATO SALAD

6 medium potatoes, washed &
    scrubbed, cooked,
    peeled and diced
1/2 cup chopped celery
1/4 cup cleaned, chopped green
    onions
2 TBSP chopped parsley
1 tsp. salt
1/8 tsp. pepper
} Mix together in a large bowl.

1 cup ranch dressing
1 TBSP Dijon mustard
} In a small bowl, mix together well.

2 hard-boiled eggs, finely chopped
Paprika

Pour dressing over potato mixture and toss to combine. Cover and refrigerate several hours.
Just before serving, sprinkle eggs and paprika over mixture.

RICKSHAW SALAD

12 ounces long spaghetti
1 tsp. salt
2 TBSP olive oil

Fill a large pot about 3/4 full with water. Add salt and olive oil. Bring to a full boil. Break spaghetti in half and drop into the water. Stir to distribute spaghetti. Turn off heat and cover pot with a tight fitting lid. Let set for 20 minutes. Drain into a large colander and rinse with cold water.

3/4 cup mayonnaise
1/4 cup soy sauce
1 tsp. salt
1/2 cup sliced water chestnuts, drained
2 (2 ounce) cans sliced mushrooms, drained
1 cup frozen peas, thawed
1/2 cup diced celery
1/2 cup chopped green pepper
1/2 cup chopped onion
1/2 tsp. garlic powder
1 (16 ounce) can bean sprouts, drained

Mix all together in a large bowl. Add spaghetti and toss lightly.

Cover and chill in the refrigerator several hours or overnight.

SOUTHWESTERN CORNBREAD SALAD

1 (6 ounce) pkg. cornbread mix } Prepare and bake according to package directions. Cool and crumble into a large bowl. Set aside.

6 slices crisp bacon, crumbled } To cook in microwave, place two paper towels on a paper plate. Lightly spray towel with cooking spray then arrange bacon on the towel in a row. Spray one side of a paper towel, place sprayed side on top of bacon, then add another towel. Cook until crisp. According to microwave wattage, it will take 3 to 5 minutes for bacon to become crisp.

1 (1 ounce) pkg. dry Buttermilk Ranch Dressing Mix } In a small bowl, mix according to pkg. directions.

1 small head romaine or iceberg lettuce, shredded
1 (15 ounce) can Mexican whole kernel corn, drained
3 large tomatoes, chopped
1 (15 ounce) can black beans, drained & rinsed
1 (16 ounce) pkg. grated Mexican 4 cheese blend
5 green onions, chopped
} Wash all vegetables and drain on paper towels before preparing. Use, in order, according to the directions below.

In a large, clear glass bowl, layer half the cornbread, bacon, lettuce, corn, tomatoes, beans, onions and cheese. Pour half the dressing over the top. Repeat layering with remaining ingredients following order given.
Cover and chill in refrigerator at least 2 hours before serving.

SPICY COLE SLAW

1 pkg. coleslaw mix
1 cup grated carrots

} Mix together in a large bowl and set aside.

1 cup salad dressing (such as
        Miracle Whip or
        Hellmann's)
2 TBSP vinegar
2 TBSP sugar or sugar substitute
1 1/2 tsp. Old Bay Seasoning

} Mix well in a small bowl and pour over slaw and carrots. Toss to mix.

Cover and chill in the refrigerator at least 2 hours before serving.

SPINACH SALAD

1 1/2 pounds fresh spinach
6 slices bacon

} Wash and dry spinach.
Cook bacon, drain and crumble.
Set aside.

3 TBSP vinegar
1/4 cup dried parsley
10 TBSP salad oil
2 tsp. Dijon mustard
1 clove garlic, minced
1/2 tsp. salt
1/2 tsp. pepper

} Combine in a small bowl, mixing well.

2 hard-cooked eggs, peeled and chopped

Just before serving, add spinach, bacon and eggs together in a large serving bowl. Pour vinegar-salad oil mixture over the top and toss together.

STRAWBERRY JELLO SALAD

1 (3 ounce) pkg. strawberry jello 1 cup boiling water	}	In a large bowl, dissolve jello in boiling water. Stir well. Let cool.

1 large can crushed pineapple
     with juice
1 (10 ounce) pkg. frozen
     strawberries, thawed
1 cup chopped pecans
2 large bananas, mashed
	}	Add to jello mixture.

1/2 pint (1 cup) sour cream

Pour half the jello mixture in a square glass container and chill in refrigerator until firm. Spread sour cream over jello. Spoon remaining jello mixture over the sour cream and refrigerate over night.

THREE BEAN SALAD

2 tsp. salt 1/4 cup sugar 1/4 cup vinegar 3/4 cup salad oil (refer to Can't Boil Water #14)	}	In a glass jar, dissolve salt and sugar in vinegar. Add salad oil. Cover and shake well.
1 can cut green beans, drained 1 can cut wax beans, drained 1 can kidney beans, drained 3/4 cup chopped celery 1/4 cup diced pimento	}	Mix together in a container that has a lid.

Pour dressing mixture over the bean mixture.
Cover and chill in the refrigerator several hours or overnight. Stir occasionally.

TWENTY-FOUR HOUR FRUIT SALAD

2 eggs, slightly beaten
2 TBSP sugar
Juice of 1 lemon
1/4 cup whipping cream

} In a heavy saucepan, stir together ingredients and cook on medium heat until thick. Stir constantly.

1 cup whipping cream

} In a large bowl, whip cream until thick and fold into egg mixture.

1 large can pineapple chunks, drained
1 large can fruit cocktail, drained
2 cups miniature marshmallows

} Fold into mixture.

Cover and let set in refrigerator 24 hours before serving.

WHIPPED LIME JELLO SALAD

1 (3 ounce) pkg. lime jello
1/2 cup boiling water
1/2 cup cold water

} In a medium bowl, dissolve jello in boiling water. Add cold water and refrigerate until mixture begins to congeal.
Using an electric mixer, whip jello until fluffy.

1/4 cup mayonnaise
1 cup cottage cheese
1 small can crushed pineapple
1/2 cup chopped pecans

} Blend into whipped jello.

Cover and refrigerate until firm.

WILTED LETTUCE SALAD

2 to 3 large bunches garden leaf or Romaine lettuce	Wash and dry lettuce. Wrap in a tea towel and keep in vegetable drawer in refrigerator until ready to use.
6 slices bacon	In a medium skillet, cook bacon until crisp. Drain on paper towels. Reserve bacon drippings from skillet for later use.
6 green onions, cleaned 1 hard-cooked egg	In a small bowl, slice onions, including tops. Chop egg into bowl with the onions. Set aside.
1 tsp. sugar 2 TBSP vinegar 1 tsp. salt 1/4 tsp. pepper	Mix ingredients with bacon drippings and heat in a medium saucepan. Do not boil.

Tear lettuce into bite size pieces into a large serving bowl. Top with egg, onion and crumbled bacon. Pour hot mixture over everything. Toss and serve immediately.

ZIP SALAD

1 (16 ounce) jar applesauce 1 (3 ounce) pkg. lime jello 1 cup bottle 7-Up	In a medium saucepan, bring applesauce to a boil. Remove from heat and add jello. Stir until dissolved. Add 7-Up. Stir well.

Pour into a mold lightly sprayed with cooking spray. Chill in the refrigerator until firm.
Serve on lettuce with mayonnaise.

This is a tart salad and good with meat.

SOUPS

CANADIAN CHEESE SOUP

1/4 cup butter 2 TBSP minced onion	} Melt butter in a heavy saucepan. Add onion and cook until clear.
1/2 cup thinly sliced carrots 3/4 cup thinly chopped celery 1 cup chicken broth	Wash vegetables and drain. Peel carrots using a vegetable peeler. Add to onion mixture and simmer gently until vegetables are tender, about 15 minutes.
1/4 cup flour 3 cups milk 2 cups grated cheese	Combine flour with one cup milk and add to the vegetable mixture, stirring constantly, until smooth and thickened. Add cheese and stir over low heat until melted.

Gradually add remaining milk, stirring briskly. Heat only to serving temperature. That is, do not let it boil.

Can't Boil Water #15: One cup of hot water and one chicken bouillon cube may be used for a chicken stock substitute.

CHEESY CREAM OF SQUASH SOUP

1 1/2 pounds yellow squash

} Wash, but do not peel. Thinly slice and set aside.

2 TBSP butter
1 medium onion, peeled & sliced
1/4 lemon, sliced, seeds removed
1/4 cup flour
6 cups chicken broth
1 tsp. salt
1/4 tsp. white pepper

} In a large saucepan, melt butter. Gently sauté onion and lemon. Sprinkle with flour and cook slowly, stirring, until flour is absorbed. Add chicken broth gradually, then sliced squash, salt and pepper. Simmer for 1 hour. Pureé soup in a blender or food processor.

1 can cream of cheese soup
Dash ground nutmeg

} Add to mixture and stir well. At this point, the mixture can be refrigerated until ready to serve.

1 cup heavy cream

To prepare for serving, stir in the heavy cream with a wire whisk and cook over low heat. Do not allow to boil.

Very good served with Cabbage Patch Bread page 77.

CHEESY POTATO SOUP

1 pkg. frozen hash brown
        potatoes, thawed
1 can cream of chicken soup
1/4 pound Velveeta cheese, cut
        into 1" chunks
	In a medium saucepan, cover
	potatoes with water. Add soup.
	Cook on medium heat for about
	30 minutes, stirring occasionally.
	Remove from heat. Stir in cheese
	and let it melt.

Refrigerate unused portion in a covered dish.

CHICKEN TORTILLA SOUP

2 TBSP vegetable cooking oil 2 cloves garlic, chopped 1 medium onion, cleaned & sliced thin, then cut in half	In a large, heavy, saucepan heat oil over medium heat. Add onions and garlic. Cook, stirring until softened.

2 small yellow squash,
        washed & sliced
2 small zucchini, washed & sliced
4 cans chicken broth
1 can diced tomatoes with juice
1 can whole kernel corn
1 TBSP Herbal Pizza & Pasta
        Magic (on spice isle in
        grocery store)
	Add squash and zucchini and cook
	about 2 minutes. Add remaining
	ingredients and bring to a boil.
	Reduce heat to low and simmer 15
	minutes.

Corn or flour tortillas, cut in strips
Fresh cilantro, chopped

Serve soup topped with some tortilla strips and fresh cilantro.

FOUR BEAN SALSA SOUP

1/2 pound sausage

} Crumble into a heavy skillet and cook until sausage begins to brown. Drain well.

1 can kidney beans
2 cans white beans
2 jars ready-made salsa
1 can black beans
1 clove garlic, peeled & minced
1 small onion, cleaned & chopped

} Place all ingredients into a large cooking pot. Mix in sausage. Cover and reduce heat and simmer 5 to 10 minutes.

1 cup Mexican four cheese blend

Pour soup into individual serving dishes and garnish with the cheese.

KING RANCH SOUP

2 cans cream of chicken soup
2 1/2 cups milk
1 (10 ounce) can green chili
    enchilada sauce
1 can Rotel tomatoes with chilies,
    drained
1 can cream of celery soup
8 ounce chopped green chilies,
    drained

} Mix and simmer in a large saucepan 5 minutes or so. Will scorch, so stir.

2 chicken breasts, cooked & diced
1 (8.75 ounce) can whole corn,
    drained

} Add to first mixture and simmer until hot.

Tortilla chips
Grated cheese

Fill individual soup bowls half full. Add 2 or 3 tortilla chips then ladle more soup on top. Cover with cheese and top with tortillas.

OLD FASHIONED SOUP

2 pounds soup or stew meat
1 cup flour
1 tsp. salt
1/2 tsp. pepper
1/4 cup cooking oil or shortening

In a heavy skillet, heat oil on medium-high. Put flour, salt and pepper into a 1 quart ziploc bag. Add meat, a small amount at a time. Shake to coat meat. Drop into skillet. Repeat until all meat is used. Brown on all sides.

4 cups water
1 cup diced carrots
1 cup diced potatoes
3/4 cup chopped celery with
        leaves
1 medium onion, sliced thin
2 cups canned tomatoes
1/2 cup rice

Clean and peel carrots, potatoes and onion. Wash celery and dry well with a paper towel. Place everything in a large pot. Bring to a high simmer. Using a slotted spoon, drain meat over skillet and transfer meat to pot. Cook until vegetables are tender.

POTATO SOUP MIX in a JAR

1 3/4 cups instant mashed
        potatoes
2 TBSP instant chicken bullion
        granules
1/4 tsp. ground white pepper
1/8 tsp. turmeric
1 1/2 tsp. seasoning salt
1 1/2 cups dry milk
2 tsp. dried minced onion
1 tsp. dried parsley
1/4 tsp. dried thyme

Combine all ingredients in a large bowl and mix well. Place in a 1 quart jar, with a screw on lid, to store.

INSTRUCTIONS TO ATTACH TO JAR:
        To Serve: Place 1/2 cup mix in soup bowl. Add 1 cup hot water. Stir until smooth.

SANTA FE SOUP

1 pound ground beef
1 pkg. taco seasoning
1 pkg. ranch dressing

} In a large, heavy skillet, brown meat and drain. Return to skillet and add both dry seasonings. Mix well.

1 can diced Rotel tomatoes
XL can tomato juice
1 can corn, drained
1 can Mexican stewed tomatoes
1 small can green chilies

} Add to meat mixture. It may be necessary to add more tomato juice for the desired consistency. Simmer at least 1 hour.

1 regular pkg. Doritoes
1 cup grated 4 cheese Mexican blend

Serve over Doritoes and garnish with cheese, avocados and/or sour cream.

ULTIMATE BAKED POTATO SOUP

3 pounds potatoes
1 1/2 cups finely chopped onions
2 TBSP minced garlic
4 TBSP butter

} Wash and scrub bake potatoes. Pierce on top with a sharp fork. Wrap in foil and bake 30 minutes in 400⁰ oven or until tender. Cool enough to handle and peel. In a bowl, cut into chunks. Melt butter in a 4 to 6 quart pot over medium-low heat. Stir in onions and garlic. Cover and cook 10 minutes until soft but not brown. Add 2/3 cup potatoes and mash with potato masher.

1 (14 ounce) can chicken broth
3 cups milk
1 tsp. salt
1/4 tsp. pepper

} Add to first mixture. Bring to a simmer stirring occasionally.

3 cups grated cheese
8 slices cooked, crumbled bacon

Add remaining potatoes and stir gently to reheat.
Garnish with cheese and bacon.

BREADS

BAKING TIPS

~ Always cover the top of a bowl with a clean tea towel (this is a light weight, white cotton cloth) when letting dough rise. Place the bowl in a warm place on the cabinet away from any direct blowing air.

~ When testing loaves of bread to see if they are done, rap on the top of the loaf with your knuckles. You should hear a hollow sound if the bread is done.

~ Most of the recipes in this book use butter. If it is in the ingredient list in a recipe, unless stated otherwise in the instructions, margarine can be substituted for the butter.

~ Party Bread is a miniature size loaf of bread. It is usually Rye or Pumpernickel and sliced thin. It is mainly used with appetizers.

~ To be sure oven temperature is correct, it is recommended to use an oven thermometer. It can be purchased at most cooking shops or hardware stores.

~ A handy tool to have are kitchen shears. They are a heavy duty pair of scissors that can be purchased at most cooking shops or hardware stores.

ANADAMA BREAD

1 1/2 cups water 1/3 cup yellow cornmeal 1 tsp. salt 1/3 cup molasses 1 1/2 tsp. cooking oil	Combine 1/2 cup water and cornmeal. In a small saucepan, bring 1 cup water and salt to a boil. Stir in cornmeal mixture and cook 2 minutes or until thick. Remove from heat. Stir in molasses and oil. Cool.
3 cups flour 1 pkg. fast acting dry yeast	Combine flour and yeast, then add to cornmeal mixture.

At the point before combining flour, yeast and cornmeal mixture, you can use a bread machine. Follow manufactory's instructions for placing ingredients in pan. OR complete instructions, then grease a 8.5" x 4.5" x 2.5" bread pan, place mixture in it and let rise until double. Bake in a 375^0 oven for 1 hour. Cool on a wire rack. Store in a ziploc bag.

Can't Boil Water #16: 2 1/4 tsp. yeast = 1 package yeast.

Do not mix fast acting yeast with water. Mix it in with the dry ingredients.
When mixing regular yeast, test water temperature with your finger. If it's too hot to touch, it's too hot for the yeast. Use only warm water (if necessary use a candy thermometer and heat water to 105^0 to 115^0.)

APRICOT-RAISIN BREAD

1 1/2 cups apricot nectar
1 1/2 cups raisins
1/3 cup cut-up dried apricots
1 TBSP grated orange peel

} In a large saucepan, combine ingredients. Simmer for 5 minutes. Cool.

2 3/4 cups flour
1 cup sugar
2 tsp. soda
1 tsp. salt
1 TBSP shortening
1 egg, slightly beaten
1/3 cup whipping cream
1/2 cup chopped walnuts

} In a large bowl, combine flour, sugar, soda, salt. Blend with a wire whisk. Add remaining ingredients, then fruit mixture. Mix, using a large spoon, until well blended.

Pour into a well greased 8.5" x 4.5" x 2.5" loaf pan. Bake in a 325⁰ oven for 80 to 90 minutes or until toothpick inserted in center comes out clean. Remove from pan. Cool on wire rack. Store in ziploc bag.

BAKING MIX BISCUITS

3 cups buttermilk baking mix
(recipe for mix, page 74)
2 1/4 tsp. quick rising dry yeast
1 cup milk

} Combine baking mix and yeast. Heat milk in microwave 30 seconds to 1 minute. Do not let it boil. test milk with your finger to make sure it is not too hot. Pour 3/4 cup milk into dry mixture. If it is too dry, add a small amount of milk until mixture is moist.

Grease a cookie sheet with shortening. Spoon mixture onto floured pastry cloth and knead a few times. Pat dough out to 1/2" thickness. Cut into 2 1/2" biscuits and place onto cookie sheet, sides touching. Lightly cover biscuits with waxed paper, then cover with plastic wrap and freeze for several hours or overnight. Let thaw before cooking. They can still be cold to the touch.
Bake in a 450⁰ oven for 15 to 18 minutes or until golden.

Can't Boil Water #17: If you like biscuits with a nice brown crust, turn them over about 5 minutes before they are done.

BANANA TEA BREAD

1 3/4 cups flour
3/4 tsp. soda
1 1/4 tsp. cream of tartar
1/2 tsp. salt
} In a large bowl, sift all together and set aside.

2 eggs
1/3 cup shortening
2 medium-size ripe bananas
2/3 cup sugar
} Place in a blender container and blend for 15 seconds or until all ingredients are blended.

Pour liquid mixture into dry ingredients. Stir until well blended. Pour into a well greased 8 1/2" x 4 1/2" x 2 1/2" loaf pan.
Bake in a 350⁰ oven for 45 minutes.
Cool on a wire rack, then store in a ziploc bag.

BREAD MUFFINS

2 cups flour
3 tsp. baking powder
1/2 tsp. salt
2 TBSP sugar
} Sift flour onto a paper plate. Measure 2 cups into the sifter and add baking powder, salt and sugar. Sift into a large mixing bowl.

1 egg
1 cup milk
1/4 cup melted shortening
} Beat egg and add milk and shortening. Stir well.

Add liquids to dry ingredients and stir just enough to moisten. Grease a 12 cup muffin pan and fill each cup 2/3's full with batter .
Bake in a 425⁰ oven for 20 minutes.
Remove from pan immediately and serve hot.

BUTTERMILK BAKING MIX

9 cups flour
2 cups whole wheat flour
1/4 cup baking powder
1 1/2 TBSP salt
1/2 cup sugar
1 cup dry powdered buttermilk
2 1/2 tsp. baking soda
2 cup shortening

}

In a very large bowl, mix dry ingredients using a wire whisk. Add shortening and mix with an electric mixer until mixture resembles cornmeal and is uniform in size.

Store in a tightly covered container on the pantry shelf.
Makes 13 cups of mix.
Storage life is 3 months.

BUTTERMILK-OATMEAL ROLLS

3/4 cup regular oats
1/2 cup boiling water
1 TBSP sugar

}

Combine in a small bowl. Stir until well blended. Let stand 5 minutes.

1 pkg. dry yeast
1 1/2 tsp. sugar
1/4 cup warm water

}

In a large bowl, dissolve yeast and sugar in water. Let stand 5 minutes.

2 1/4 cups bread flour,
       reserve 1/2 cup
1/4 cup buttermilk
1 TBSP butter, melted
3/4 tsp. salt

}

Spoon 1 3/4 cups flour into yeast mixture along with oat mixture, buttermilk, butter and salt. Stir to form a soft dough.

Using some of the 1/2 cup reserved flour, spread it on a pastry cloth. Turn dough out onto surface. Knead until smooth and elastic adding enough of the remaining flour, 1 TBSP at a time, to prevent dough from sticking to hands. Dough will be slightly sticky. Place dough in a lightly greased large bowl, cover with a tea towel. Let rise in a warm place 45 minutes. Punch dough down, cover and let rest 5 minutes. Divide dough into 12 equal pieces. Shape each one into a ball. Place in a lightly greased 9" square pan. Cover and let rise 30 minutes. Bake in a 375^0 oven for 25 minutes. Brush melted butter over tops. Serve warm.

CABBAGE PATCH BREAD

1 pkg. dry yeast
1/3 cup warm water

} In a large mixing bowl, dissolve yeast in water. Set aside.

1 (5 ounce) can evaporated milk
1/4 cup cooking oil
1 egg
3/4 cup coarsely chopped cabbage
1 carrot, cut up
1/4 cup sliced celery
1/4 cup snipped parsley
2 TBSP honey
1 tsp. salt

} In a blender or food processor, combine ingredients. Blend until smooth.
Add to yeast mixture.

3 cups whole wheat flour
1 1/4 cups white flour

} Using a wooden spoon, stir in whole wheat flour and then as much white flour as possible to make a soft but workable dough. Do not use too much white flour at this point.

Turn dough out onto lightly floured pastry cloth. Knead in enough remaining flour to make moderately stiff dough that is smooth and elastic.
Shape into a ball and place in a large greased bowl, turning once. Cover with a tea towel and let rise until double (about 1 1/4 hours).
Punch down then divide dough in half. Cover and let rest on pastry cloth 10 minutes.
Shape dough into 2 round loaves. Place on greased baking sheet. Cover and let rise until double (about 30 minutes).
Bake in a 350^0 oven for 30 minutes or until done. If necessary, cover with foil last 10 minutes to prevent over browning.
Cool on wire racks.
Store in large ziploc bags and refrigerate. Can be frozen.

Very good served with soft cream cheese, pimento cheese, tuna or chicken salad.

CHEESE & GARLIC BREAD

1 large loaf Italian bread 4 TBSP butter 1/3 cup grated mozzarella cheese 4 cloves garlic, chopped	Cut loaf in half lengthwise. Spread each half with softened butter. Sprinkle cheese and garlic evenly over each bread half.
1/4 cup grated Parmesan cheese 1 tsp. dried basil 1 tsp. dried parsley 1/2 tsp. crushed red pepper flakes	In a small bowl, mix ingredients together. Sprinkle over top of bread.

Place bread halves on an ungreased baking sheet.
Bake in a preheated 350⁰ oven for 15 minutes or until cheese is melted and bread is golden. Cool slightly. Cut into 1" thick slices. Serve immediately.

CHEESE BREAD STICKS

2 cups buttermilk biscuit mix 1 cup grated sharp cheese 3/4 cup milk	In a large bowl, stir mix and cheese together. Stir in just enough milk to make a soft, but not sticky dough.

2 to 3 TBSP poppy seeds

Turn dough out onto a lightly floured pastry cloth and knead a few times.
Roll pieces of dough between palms to form pencil-like shapes about 1/2" in diameter and 4" long. Roll dough in poppy seeds.
Bake in a pre-heated 450⁰ oven for 10 minutes.

CHEESE CRUMB MUFFINS

1 1/3 cups flour
4 tsp. baking powder
3/4 tsp salt
1/3 cup sugar
1 1/3 cups corn flake crumbs
    (see Can't Boil Water #34)

In a medium bowl, stir together first 4 ingredients. Stir in crumbs and set aside.

1 egg
1 1/2 cups milk
1/3 cup cooking oil
1/2 cup grated cheese

In a large mixing bowl, beat egg until foamy. Stir in milk and oil. Add first mixture and cheese, mixing well.

Let stand 2 minutes. Spoon batter evenly into 12 greased muffin tins.
Bake in a 400⁰ oven for 25 minutes or until lightly browned.

CHEESE PINWHEEL ROLLS

1 pkg. yeast roll mix (makes 18)

Make according to directions on package. Let rise in a large bowl covered with a damp cloth until double in bulk (about 45 minutes).

1 1/2 cups grated sharp cheese
2 tsp. nutmeg
Paprika
3 TBSP butter, melted

Punch dough down in the bowl, then turn out onto a lightly floured pastry cloth. Knead until smooth, elastic and easy to handle. Roll out dough into a 12" x 18" rectangle. Sprinkle cheese over entire top of dough. Roll up like a jelly roll starting from the long side. Pinch edge together along roll. Cut into 1" slices. Place cut side up in greased muffin tins. Cut a cross about 1/2" deep on top of each roll with kitchen shears (heavy duty scissors). Sprinkle with spices. Brush with melted butter. Cover with a damp cloth and let rise until double in bulk (about 45 minutes).
Bake in a pre-heated 375⁰ oven for 20 minutes.

CHEESY CHIP ROLLS

Grease 12 muffin cups

1 cup potato chips, crushed
1/2 cup slivered almonds
1/2 cup grated Parmesan cheese
} Combine in a small bowl and set aside.

2 (8 ounce) cans refrigerated dinner rolls
1/2 cup Italian salad dressing
} Separate dough from each can into twelve pieces. Dip each piece in salad dressing, then coat both sides with chip mixture. Stand two rolls on edge in each muffin cup. Sprinkle rolls with any remaining potato chip mixture.

Bake in a 375⁰ oven for 15 to 20 minutes or until rolls are golden brown. Serve hot.

CORNMEAL-CHEDDAR MUFFINS

Preheat oven to 350⁰

1 3/4 cups flour
1/4 cup yellow cornmeal
1 1/2 tsp. baking powder
1/4 tsp. salt
1/8 tsp. ground red pepper
3 TBSP chilled, butter, cut into small pieces
1/3 cup grated cheddar cheese
} Combine first 6 ingredients in a large bowl, stirring with a whisk. Cut in butter with a pastry blender until mixture resembles coarse meal. Stir in cheese.

1 cup buttermilk
1/4 cup water
1 large egg, lightly beaten
} In a medium bowl, combine with the whisk and add to dry mixture, stirring with a spoon just until moistened.

Spray a 12 cup muffin pan with cooking spray. Divide batter evenly among cups.
Bake for 30 minutes or until muffins spring back when touched lightly in center.
Store cold muffins in a ziploc bag up to two days or freeze up to 3 months.

ENERGY BARS

3 to 3 1/2 cups flour
1/4 cup sugar
1 pkg. quick rising yeast
1 tsp. salt

> In a large bowl, combine 1 1/2 cups flour with sugar, yeast and salt.

1/2 cup milk
1/2 cup water
1/4 cup butter

> In a small micro-safe bowl, heat together in microwave until very warm. Butter does not need to melt. Stir into dry ingredients.

1/2 cup chopped pecans
1 cup total of assorted dried
        fruits, such as
        raisins, cranberries,
        cherries, blueberries
        or chopped dried
        apricots

> Stir into dough mixture.

Stir in enough of the remaining flour to make soft dough. Knead on a lightly floured pastry cloth until smooth and elastic. Cover and let rest 10 minutes. Roll or press dough to a 12" circle. Place on greased pizza pan or large baking sheet. Cover and let rise in warm, draft-free place until almost doubled in size (about 25 minutes).
Bake in a 400⁰ oven for 15 to 20 minutes or until done. Remove from pan and cool on a wire rack.
To serve, cut into 12 wedges.
Store wedges in ziploc bags.
Great to carry out for a snack.

IRISH SODA BREAD

4 cups flour
1/4 cup sugar
1 tsp. salt
1 tsp. baking powder
2 TBSP caraway seed
1/4 cup butter
2 cups raisins

} Sift 1st four ingredients together into a large bowl, then stir in caraway seeds. Cut in butter, using a pastry blender, until mixture resembles coarse corn meal. Stir in raisins.

1 1/3 cups buttermilk
1 egg, slightly beaten
1 tsp. soda

} In a small bowl, combine and add to dry mixture just until moistened.

1 TBSP whipping cream

Knead dough lightly on a floured pastry cloth until smooth. Shape into a ball. Place in a greased 2 quart casserole dish. Make a 4" cross, 1/4" deep, in top of loaf. Brush with cream. Bake in a 375^0 oven for 1 hour. Cool before slicing.

MEXICAN CORNBREAD

1 1/2 cups cornmeal
1/2 cup flour
4 tsp. baking powder
1 tsp. salt
1/2 tsp. soda
3/4 cup milk
1 small can cream-style corn
1 large onion, chopped fine
Dash garlic powder
3 jalapeño peppers,
        seeds removed, chopped fine
1/3 cup cooking oil

} Mix all ingredients together in a large bowl.

1/2 pound cheese, grated

Pour half the mixture into a 12" greased round baking pan. Sprinkle all the cheese on top. Pour remaining mixture over cheese.
Bake in a 350^0 oven for 45 minutes or until golden brown.

Can't Boil Water #18: The Mexican cornbread is best baked in a heavy iron skillet.

OATMEAL HURRY-UPS

1 1/4 cups flour
3 tsp. baking powder
1/2 tsp. salt
1 1/2 cups oatmeal
3 TBSP shortening, melted
1 cup milk

} In a large bowl, combine 1st four ingredients using a whisk. Combine cooled shortening and milk. Stir into dry ingredients just enough to moisten.

Drop by teaspoonful on a well-greased large cookie sheet.
Bake in a 450^0 oven for 15 minutes.

POPOVERS

2 eggs
1 cup milk

} In a medium mixing bowl, beat eggs then add milk. Beat until light and fluffy with a whisk.

1 cup flour
1/2 tsp. salt

} Combine and beat into egg mixture.

1 TBSP shortening, melted

Heat oven to 450^0.
Divide melted shortening evenly into 8 large popover cups. Place in oven for 1 minute. Remove and fill each cup half full with batter.
Bake for 30 minutes (Do not open oven door).
Reduce heat to 350^0 and bake 15 minutes longer.
Serve immediately.

HINT: A popover pan is necessary and can be purchased at a cooking shop or on the internet.

PUFF BALL COFFEE CAKE

1/2 cup sugar
1/2 tsp. cinnamon
1/2 cup chopped nuts

} Mix together in a small bowl and set aside.

2 pkgs. canned biscuits
1/3 cup butter, melted

} Shape each biscuit into a ball. Dip into melted butter, then into the sugar mixture.

Arrange balls in 2 layers in a greased tube pan or Bundt pan.
Bake in a 375⁰ oven for 25 minutes.
Remove from pan onto a large plate and serve immediately.

PUMPKIN LOAF BREAD

Makes two loaves.

2 cups flour
1 1/3 cups whole wheat flour
2 1/2 tsp. pumpkin pie spice
1 1/2 tsp. baking powder
1 1/2 tsp. salt
1 tsp. baking soda
1 3/4 cups sugar

} Combine in a large bowl using a whisk.

1/2 cup shortening
4 eggs
1 (15 ounce) can pumpkin pureé
1/2 cup honey
1/3 cup water
1 cup chopped pecans or walnuts

} Mix together 1st five ingredients in a medium bowl, then beat into dry ingredients. Stir in nuts.

Grease the inside of the bottom and 1/2" up insides of 2 loaf pans. Divide mixture into the pans.
Bake in a 350⁰ oven for 55 minutes.

SHORTCAKE BISCUITS

2 cups buttermilk baking mix
              (recipe page 74)
1/4 cup sugar
3/4 cup milk
1 egg

Place baking mix and sugar into a medium size mixing bowl. Stir together.
Break the egg into a 1 cup measuring cup and slightly beat. Add enough milk to the egg to make 3/4 cup. Stir everything together to form a soft dough.

Knead on a lightly floured pastry cloth several times. Roll dough 1/2" thick. Cut with a large biscuit cutter. Place on lightly greased baking sheet.
Bake in a 450⁰ oven for 10 to 12 minutes.
While biscuits are still hot, split and butter both sides then put together again until serving time.
To serve, place bottom half in a small serving bowl. Top with sweetened fruit.
Place biscuit top over fruit and top with whipping cream.

SODA POP BISCUITS

2 cups buttermilk baking mix
              (recipe page 74
1 TBSP sugar
1/2 cup sour cream
1/2 cup lemon-lime soda pop
1/4 cup butter, melted

In a medium mixing bowl, combine mix and sugar. Add sour cream and soda pop just enough to moisten dry ingredients.

Spoon onto a floured pastry cloth and knead several times. Roll or pat out to 1/2" thick. Cut with a biscuit cutter. Spread half the melted butter on a medium sized baking sheet. Place biscuits on baking sheet and brush tops with remaining butter.
Bake in a 450⁰ oven for 15 to 20 minutes.

SOPAPILLAS

4 cups flour
4 tsp. baking powder
1 tsp. salt
1 TBSP shortening

} Mix dry ingredients together in a large bowl. Using your hands, mix in shortening

1 egg, beaten
1 cup water

} Add to first mixture to form a stiff dough. Knead well.

Shortening for deep frying

Divide dough into four parts. Roll each part 1/8" thick on a lightly floured pastry cloth. Cut into 3" square pieces. Fry in hot deep fat. Turn often so they will puff evenly. Drain on paper towels.
Serve with butter and honey.

Can't Boil Water #19: It is best to use an electric deep fryer, but a deep cast iron skillet or pot will do.

SOUR CREAM BREAD

1 pkg. dry yeast
1/2 cup warm water

} In a large bowl, dissolve yeast in water. Let set about 5 minutes.

1 egg
1 cup sour cream
2 tsp. sugar
2 1/3 cups self-rising flour

} In a small bowl, stir together egg and sour cream. Set aside. In a medium bowl, stir sugar into flour. Set aside. Add alternately to yeast and mix well.

Pour into a greased 8.5" x 4.5" x 2.5" loaf pan. Let rise for 50 minutes.
Bake in a 350⁰ oven for 45 minutes.

SPOON ROLLS

1 pkg. dry yeast 2 cups warm water	} In a large bowl, dissolve yeast in the warm water. Let stand 5 minutes.
3/4 cup butter, softened 4 cups self-rising flour	} Combine with yeast mixture.
1 egg, slightly beaten 1/4 cup sugar	} Stir into batter. Mixture will be soft.

Cover tightly and refrigerate overnight. Spoon batter into greased muffin pans, filling 2/3 full. Let rise for about 30 minutes.
Bake in a 375^0 oven for 25 minutes.

NOTE: Batter may be stored, covered, in refrigerator up to 4 days.

THREE for ONE

Makes three loaves.

2 cups milk 1/2 cup butter 1 tsp. salt 1/2 cup sugar	} In a medium saucepan, stir ingredients together and heat to combine . Do not let boil. Set aside to cool to lukewarm.
6 1/2 cups flour 1 pkg. quick rising yeast	} Mix 1/2 cup flour with yeast and add to liquid mixture. Gradually stir in remaining flour and continue stirring until mixture forms a dough.

Cover and let dough rise one hour. Spoon out onto a floured pastry cloth and knead. Divide into three parts. Roll each third into a rectangle. Then, starting at one end, roll up dough jelly-roll fashion and seal ends by pressing under. Place each loaf in a greased loaf pan. Let rise 45 minutes.
Bake in a 375^0 oven for 50 to 60 minutes. Brush tops with melted butter.

TOMATO BREAD

2 cups tomato juice 2 TBSP butter 3 TBSP sugar 1 tsp. salt 1/4 cup ketchup	In a medium saucepan, heat tomato juice and butter until butter melts. Add sugar, salt and ketchup, then stir. Cool until lukewarm.
1 pkg. dry yeast 1/4 cup warm water 7 cups flour	In a large bowl, sprinkle yeast over warm water. Stir to dissolve. Add tomato mixture and 3 cups flour. Beat with electric mixer two minutes at medium speed. Using a rubber spatula, scrape bowl occasionally. Mix in enough remaining flour to make a soft dough.

Turn dough onto a lightly floured pastry cloth and knead until smooth and elastic. Place in lightly greased bowl. Turn dough to grease top. Cover and let rise in a warm place until doubled, about 1 1/2 hours. Punch down and divide in half. Cover and let rest 10 minutes on pastry cloth. Shape into 2 loaves and place in greased 8.5" x 4.5" x 2.5" loaf pans. Cover and let rise about 1 hour. Bake in a 425⁰ oven for 25 minutes.

WHOLE WHEAT PIZZA CRUST

1 pkg. dry yeast
1/4 cup warm water
1 cup whole wheat flour
1/4 tsp. salt
1/2 to 2/3 cup warm water
1 cup white flour
1 TBSP olive oil

Dissolve yeast in 1/4 cup warm water in a small bowl. Let stand 5 minutes. In a large bowl, combine flours and salt. Stir the yeast mixture and oil into the flour mixture. Add enough warm water to make a moderate stiff dough. Stir well. Cover and let stand 15 minutes.

Cooking spray

Turn dough out on lightly floured pastry cloth. Knead 5 to 8 times. Divide dough in half. Roll each half in 12" circles. Place each on 12" pizza pans coated with cooking spray (if pan has holes in bottom, spray cooking spray on a paper towel then rub on pan.)
Bake in a 425⁰ oven for 5 to 8 minutes. May freeze 1 crust for later use.
Place favorite toppings on top of crust, top with pizza cheese and bake 15 to 20 minutes or until crust is brown on edge.

If using a larger pan, use all the dough and cook a few minutes longer.

YEAST CORNBREAD

1 cup milk
6 TBSP sugar
2 tsp. salt
1/2 cup butter

> In a medium saucepan, scald milk. Stir in other ingredients. Cool to lukewarm.

1/2 cup warm water
2 pkgs. dry yeast
2 eggs, beaten
3 1/2 cup flour
1 3/4 cups yellow cornmeal

> Put warm water in a large bowl and sprinkle yeast on top. Stir until dissolved. Add milk mixture to the yeast mixture and stir, then add remaining ingredients. Beat until well blended. Batter will be stiff.

Divide into two well greased 8" round cake pans. Cover and let rise in warm place until doubled in bulk (about 1 hour.)
Bake in a 375° oven for 30 to 35 minutes.
Serve warm.

Can't Boil Water #20: To scald milk, place in a heavy bottom saucepan, on low heat. Stir occasionally until milk is just hot with steam and small bubbles appear around the edges. DO NOT BOIL. Remove from the heat. This can also be done in the microwave using a micro-safe cup. For one cup of milk cook for 40-45 seconds or until warm to the touch. Just be sure to watch so the milk will not start to boil.

VEGETABLES

VEGETABLE & FRUIT TIPS

~ Cut away any damaged or bruised areas on fresh fruits and vegetables before preparing and/or eating. Produce that looks rotten should be discarded.

~ All produce should be thoroughly washed before eating. This includes produce grown conventionally or organically at home, or produce that is purchased from a grocery store or farmer's market.

~ Wash fruits and vegetables under running water just before eating, cutting or cooking. Even if you plan to peel the produce before eating, it is still important to wash it first.

~ Soak vegetables in a solution of 1 gallon of water and 2 TBSP of vinegar for 10 minutes, then rinse well.

~ Washing fruits and vegetables with soap or detergent or using commercial produce washes is not recommended.

~ Scrub firm produce, such as melons and cucumbers, with a clean produce brush.

~ Drying produce with a clean cloth towel or paper towel may further reduce bacteria that may be present.

~ Never cut vegetables or fruit on the same cutting board or with the same knife you have already used to cut meat.

BACON WRAPPED CORN on the COB

6 frozen ears of corn
6 slices bacon

} Thaw corn. Wrap a bacon slice around each ear and secure with toothpicks.

Place on a hot grill for about 20 minutes until corn is tender and bacon is crisp. Turn occasionally to cook on all sides.

BAKED CAULIFLOWER

3 slices bacon

} On a paper plate, place two paper towels, spray with cooking spray, then bacon slices. Fold two paper towels in half, spray one side with the cooking spray, then place the sprayed side down on the bacon. Cook in microwave 30 seconds per slice or until crisp. Drain on a clean paper towel. Crumble into a small bowl. Set aside.

1 medium size head cauliflower
1 1/2 cups tomato juice
1 TBSP instant minced onion
1 tsp. salt

} Wash and trim cauliflower. Separate into small sections. Place in a one quart casserole. Add tomato juice, onion and salt.

Cover tightly with foil and bake in a 375⁰ oven for 40 minutes. Sprinkle crumbled bacon on top and serve.

BAKED SPINACH

4 eggs
2/3 cup milk
1/2 cup butter
1/2 cup minced onion
2 TBSP dry parsley flakes
1 tsp. Worcestershire sauce
1 1/2 tsp. salt
1/2 tsp. thyme
1/2 tsp. nutmeg

In a medium bowl, beat eggs until creamy. Add other ingredients and mix well.

2 (10 ounce) pkgs. frozen
         chopped spinach
2 cups cooked rice
2 cups grated American cheese

Cook spinach according to package directions in a large saucepan. Drain well, then return to pan. Mix with rice and cheese. Stir well.

Combine both mixtures in the large saucepan and stir well.
Grease well a 2 quart baking dish and pour mixture into dish.
Bake in a 325⁰ oven for 1 hour.
Cut into squares to serve.

BASIC QUICHE RECIPE

Purchased pie dough for single crust pie (or) prepare using recipe on page 165)	If using purchased, let dough set out on counter, still in plastic package, about 30 minutes or until it is easy to unroll. Follow directions #21 below.
4 eggs, beaten 3/4 cup whipping cream, half & half or sour cream 1 1/4 cups milk 1 1/2 to 2 cups vegetables and/or cheese, your choice	In a large bowl, combine, mixing well. If you use vegetables, add 3/4 cup grated cheese.

Pour mixture into the baked pie shell and bake in a 375⁰ oven for 40 minutes.

Can't Boil Water #21: When baking pie crust without ingredients, lay the dough over the pie plate and ease into place, working from the center of the dough. If necessary, trim dough to hang over side 1 1/2". Fold dough over to the top of the plate and flute (a decorative edge.) Using a fork, prick the bottom of the dough. Place a square piece of non-stick foil over dough, non-stick side facing dough, and shape it to the bottom and up sides of dough, taking care not to flatten the fluted edge. Add a package of baking weights (they look like small marbles) or 2 cups of dry pinto beans to cover top of foil that's in the bottom of the pan. Bake in a 400⁰ oven for 12 minutes. Remove from oven and remove foil and marbles 3 minutes before crust is done then continue baking. This holds dough in place until it is done enough to be set.

CHEDDAR BAKED POTATOES

3 large Idaho baking potatoes

Wash and scrub potatoes and pat dry with a paper towel. Prick with a sharp fork 3 or 4 times on top. Wrap in foil and place on a cookie sheet. Bake in a 400⁰ oven for 1 hour.

1/4 cup butter
1 cup sour cream
1 TBSP grated onion
1 tsp. salt
1/2 cup grated cheddar cheese

In a medium bowl, mix first 4 ingredients together, then add cheese.

Cut hot potatoes in half lengthwise. Scoop out potato, saving shells. Whip together potatoes with cheese mixture. Divide mixture into shells. At this point, you can place filled shells on a tray in the freezer to harden, then wrap, individually, in moisture-proof wrapping and store in freezer. When ready to serve, remove wrapping, place on baking sheet and bake in 375⁰ oven for 45 minutes.
Or, you can place filled shells on the baking sheet and bake immediately in a 375⁰ oven for 20 minutes or until heated through.

CHEESE PUFFS FOR TWO

3 slices white or wheat bread
2 TBSP butter, melted
2 (10 ounce) oven-proof
    custard cups

> Brush melted butter on one side of each bread slice. Cut into strips. Divide the strips and place along the sides and in the bottom of each custard cup.

2 eggs, slightly beaten
1 cup milk
1/2 cup grated American cheese
1/4 tsp. onion salt
1/4 tsp. salt
8 drops Tabasco sauce

> In a medium size bowl, mix ingredients well. Pour equal amounts into each custard cup.

Place on a small baking sheet.
Bake in a 350⁰ oven for 35 minutes or until puffy and golden brown.
Serve immediately.

CHEESY PIZZA POTATOES

1 pound ground beef

> In a large heavy skillet, crumble and cook meat until brown. Drain well using a large strainer.

1 pkg. Au Gratin potatoes
1 cup hot water
2/3 cup milk
1/4 cup sliced, pitted ripe olives
1/2 tsp. salt
1/2 tsp. Italian Seasoning
1/4 tsp. pepper
1 (16 ounce) can whole tomatoes,
    undrained
1 (4 ounce) can mushroom stems
    & pieces, drained

> In a large bowl, break up tomatoes. Mix remaining ingredients with tomatoes and add drained beef. Mix well.

1 cup Mozzarella cheese

Pour mixture into a greased 2 quart casserole dish. Bake, uncovered, in a 400⁰ oven for 45 minutes. Sprinkle with the cheese and bake until cheese melts. (about 5 minutes).
Let stand 5 minutes before serving.

CHEESY TOMATO TART

1 crust from a 15 ounce pkg. of
    refrigerated pie
    dough

}

Press the pie dough in the bottom and up the sides of a 9" tart pan. Bake (Can't Boil Water #21) Set aside.

1 tsp. garlic juice
1 1/2 cups grated fontina cheese,
    reserve 1/2 cup
4 large tomatoes
1/2 tsp. salt
1/4 tsp. pepper

}

Slice tomatoes and place on folded paper towels. Sprinkle evenly with salt and pepper and let stand 10 minutes. Sprinkle garlic juice over pie crust and sprinkle 1/2 cup cheese on top. Arrange tomato slices over grated cheese. Sprinkle with remaining 1 cup cheese.

Bake in a 350⁰ oven for 45 minutes. Remove from oven, then slice into squares.

Can't Boil Water #22: A 9" round cake pan can be substituted for a 9" tart pan.

CHEF-BAKED CHEESE POTATOES

6 Idaho baking potatoes

Wash and scrub potatoes then pat dry with a paper towel. Punch several holes in top of each potato with a sharp fork. Wrap in foil. Place on a cookie sheet and bake in a 350⁰ oven 30 minutes or until tender.

1/2 cup sour cream
1/4 cup butter, softened
1 cup grated American cheese
2 TBSP chopped green onions

Combine ingredients in a medium bowl, mixing well.

Gently roll potatoes to soften. Make a crisscross cut on top of each potato and press ends to fluff and make top open. Fill each top with the cheese mixture. Place back on the cookie sheet and bake in a 350⁰ oven for 15 minutes. Serve hot.

Can't Boil Water #23: To test if potato is done, fold a paper towel several times being sure it is long enough to fold in half over the potato. Gently squeeze the sides of the potato. If it is done, you will be able to make a 'dent.' Don't squeeze too hard.

COTTAGE CHEESE SCALLOPED POTATOES

1 cup thinly sliced (crosswise) raw potatoes 1 cup cottage cheese	Butter a small baking dish. Arrange alternate layers of cottage cheese and potatoes.
1/2 to 3/4 cup milk Salt and pepper to taste	In a small saucepan, heat milk to a warm temperature. Do not let it boil.

Sprinkle salt and pepper over the potato mixture, then pour the heated milk on top of the seasoned potatoes. If 1/2 cup of milk is not enough to cover the potato mixture, add more until covered.

Bake in a 325° oven 25 minutes or until potatoes are tender when pierced with a fork.

CREAM CHEESE CORN

2 cups whole kernel corn, drained 1/2 tsp. onion salt 1/4 cup milk 1 TBSP butter 1 (3 ounce) pkg. cream cheese	Combine all together in a medium saucepan or electric skillet.

1/4 cup fresh parsley, chopped (optional)

Cook 20 minutes on medium heat or until well heated and cream cheese is melted.

Sprinkle with parsley and serve immediately.

DIJON POTATOES

6 medium red-skin potatoes } Wash potatoes and cut into chunks. Place in a lightly greased 9" x 13" x 2" baking dish. Set aside.

5 TBSP Dijon mustard
2 TBSP olive oil
1 clove garlic, chopped
1/2 tsp. Italian seasoning } Mix together in a small bowl.

Pour mustard mixture over potatoes and toss to coat potatoes.
Bake in a 425^0 oven for 35 minutes or until potatoes are fork tender, (Can't Boil Water #24), stirring occasionally.

EGGPLANT PIE

Pastry for 1 pie crust
1 medium eggplant, sliced with
          skin on
1 cup grated sharp cheddar cheese
2 medium tomatoes, sliced
1 medium white onion, sliced
Salt and pepper to taste } Place pastry in a 9" pie plate, fluting the edges. Layer into the prepared pie crust the eggplant, cheese, tomato and onion in the order given. Repeat process, ending with the cheese on top.

Bake in a 350^0 oven for 30 minutes. Remove from oven, and let rest 5 minutes before slicing and serving.

GINGER ASPARAGUS

1 1/2 pounds fresh asparagus
2 tsp. cooking oil

Wash asparagus and drain on paper towels. Trim bottom ends. Heat the oil on medium-high in a large non-stick skillet. Sauté asparagus for 7 minutes.

2 tsp. minced fresh ginger
1/2 tsp. sugar
1/4 tsp. salt
1/4 tsp. pepper
1 tsp. sesame oil

Add ginger to asparagus and sauté 1 minute.

Stir in remaining ingredients and cook 1 minute.
Remove from skillet and place on a serving plate. Serve immediately.

Try this recipe with fresh green beans or broccoli instead of asparagus.

HOLIDAY GREEN BEANS

3 TBSP butter
1/2 cup chopped celery
4 TBSP flour
1 cup powdered non-dairy
            creamer
2 cups boiling water
1/2 tsp. salt
1/4 tsp. pepper
1 tsp. Worcestershire sauce
3/4 cup grated Parmesan cheese
1 (5 ounce) sliced can water
            chestnuts, drained
2 (10 ounce) pkgs. frozen
      French-style green beans
            cooked and drained
2 TBSP chopped pimento

In a large saucepan, melt butter over low heat until frothy. Add celery and sauté until tender. Blend in flour. Cook and stir 1 minute. Add dry creamer, then add boiling water all at once, beating with wire whip to blend. Increase heat to moderate. Cook and stir until sauce comes to a boil and thickens. Remove from heat and add seasonings, Worcestershire and 1/2 cup cheese. Mix until cheese melts. Add water chestnuts and cooked beans, mixing lightly.

Pour into a greased, shallow, 1 quart casserole. Top with remaining cheese and chopped pimento.
Bake in a pre-heated 325⁰ oven for 30 minutes.

MAPLE SYRUP SWEET POTATOES

2 1/2 pounds sweet potatoes

} Wash and scrub and blot dry with paper towels. Peel, then cut into 1/4" thick slices. Place slices in a 2 quart casserole dish.

1/3 cup orange juice
1/4 cup maple syrup
2 TBSP brown sugar
1 TBSP butter, melted
1/2 tsp. salt
1/8 tsp. ground cloves

} Combine ingredients in a small bowl. Pour mixture over potatoes.

1/4 cup chopped pecans

} Spread pecans on a small cookie sheet and toast in a 325⁰ oven for 5 minutes. Stir two times to assure even toasting.

Cover casserole dish loosely with plastic wrap and microwave on high 5 minutes. Stir and continue cooking for 5 more minutes. Uncover and cook again for 5 minutes or until potatoes are fork tender. Sprinkle with pecans before serving.

Can't Boil Water #24 When testing vegetables with a fork to see if they are done, test close to the center of several pieces. The fork should slide in food easily.

OKRA CROQUETTES

1 egg 1 TBSP flour 3 TBSP cornmeal 1/4 tsp. salt 1/4 tsp. pepper 2 cups finely chopped okra 1/4 cup finely peeled, chopped onion	Wash the okra and cut off the top and a small portion of the tip before chopping. In a large bowl, beat egg, then add dry ingredients. Mix well and stir in okra and onion.
1/2 cup cooking oil	Heat oil in a medium size heavy skillet.

Drop okra mixture by TBSP into hot oil. Cook about 3 minutes, turn and flatten with spatula to make a croquette. Cook about 2 minutes or until brown. Drain on several layers of paper towels.

OVEN BAKED ZUCCHINI CHIPS

1/4 cup unseasoned bread crumbs 1/4 cup grated fresh Parmesan cheese 1/4 tsp. seasoned salt 1/4 tsp. garlic powder 1/8 tsp. pepper	In a small bowl, mix together with a wire whisk. Set aside.
1/4 cup milk	Place in a shallow bowl. Set aside.
2 small to medium zucchini	Wash and slice 1/4" thick.

Coat a wire rack with cooking spray (do this by hold it over the sink to keep from spraying everything else). Place rack in a cookie sheet.
Dip zucchini in milk and dredge to coat both sides in bread crumb mixture. Place slices on the coated rack.
Bake in a 425° oven for 30 minutes or until browned and crisp.
Serve immediately.

OVEN RICE
ACK's original

1 can chicken broth
1 broth can full of water
1/8 tsp. garlic powder
1 1/2 tsp. onion flakes
1/2 tsp. oregano
1 TBSP olive oil or butter
3/4 cup long grain rice

} Put ingredients into a 1 quart baking dish and stir well.

Bake in a 350⁰ oven for 1 hour.

POTATO PUFF

2 cups mashed potatoes
2 eggs
3 TBSP cream
1 TBSP butter, softened
1/2 tsp. salt

} Separate eggs (instructions on page 18) and reserve whites. Beat yolks in a small bowl and set aside. Place mashed potatoes in a large saucepan. Add beaten yolks, cream, butter and salt. Stir constantly over medium heat until light and hot. Remove from heat. Lightly beat egg white and stir in potato mixture.

Pour into a greased 1 quart casserole dish.
Bake in a pre-heated 450⁰ oven for 15 minutes or until brown on top.

POTATOES ROMANOFF

5 large Idaho potatoes } Wash and scrub, peel, dice and cook until tender in a large saucepan at medium heat using enough water to cover potatoes.

5 green onions, cleaned & chopped
1 (12 ounce) carton cottage cheese
1 (8 ounce) carton sour cream
1/2 tsp. salt
1/4 tsp. pepper
} Combine in a medium bowl and set aside.

1 cup grated cheese

Drain potatoes. Mix with onion-sour cream mixture. Place in a greased 1 1/2 quart casserole dish and top with the cheese.
Bake in a 350⁰ oven for 40 minutes.

RICE and CARROTS

1 1/2 cups grated carrots
1/2 tsp. salt
} Wash and peel carrots using a vegetable peeler. Grate into a small saucepan covered with water. Add salt and simmer 5 minutes.

1 cup cooked rice
1 egg, beaten
1 TBSP diced onion
1 cup grated cheese
} Mix all together in a medium bowl.

Drain carrots. Add to rice mixture and place in a greased 1 quart casserole dish.
Bake in a 350⁰ oven for 20 minutes.

SCALLOPED CIDER POTATOES

2 TBSP flour 1 cup milk 1 cup apple cider 1/2 cup chicken broth 1/2 tsp. salt 1/4 tsp. pepper 1/8 tsp. ground nutmeg	Place the flour in a medium saucepan. Gradually add the milk, stirring with a whisk until blended. Stir in cider, broth, salt, pepper and nutmeg. Bring to a boil over medium heat, stirring constantly. Remove from heat.
1/2 cup grated smoked Gouda cheese (can use Jack or Muenster) 1/2 cup grated Jarlsberg cheese (can use Swiss) 2 pounds Yukon gold potatoes	Combine cheeses in a small bowl and set aside. Wash and scrub then peel and thinly slice potatoes.

Arrange half the potato slices in a shallow 3 quart casserole and sprinkle with half the cheese mixture. Arrange the remaining potatoes on top. Pour the cider mixture over the potatoes and bake in a 425^0 oven for 25 minutes. Remove from oven, press potatoes with a spatula. Sprinkle remaining cheese on top and bake an additional 20 minutes or until potatoes are tender.

SCALLOPED YAMS with APRICOTS

1 cup water 1/2 cup dried apricots 1 TBSP sugar	Place into a medium saucepan, cover and cook over low heat until apricots are tender and most of the water is absorbed (about half hour).
1 (1 pound) can yams	Drain well and slice. Arrange in a 1 1/2 quart casserole. Cover with apricots.
1/8 tsp. cinnamon 1 cup dairy sour cream	In a small bowl gently blend, then spread over apricots.

Bake in a 350^0 oven for 30 minutes.

SOUR CREAM POTATOES with OLIVES

6 medium Idaho potatoes

Wash and scrub, peel, cube and cook in a medium saucepan, in enough water to cover the potatoes, until tender. Drain well.

2 cups sour cream
1/2 cup chopped pimento stuffed
olives
1/4 cup chopped black olives
1/4 cup chopped onion
1 tsp. salt
1/2 tsp. pepper
1/2 tsp paprika
1 TBSP chopped parsley

Combine all ingredients in a large bowl. Add cooked potatoes and stir well.

Place in a 2 quart casserole dish. Bake in a 350⁰ oven for 35 minutes.

SPECIAL CANDIED SWEET POTATOES

2 pounds sweet potatoes

Wash and scrub then cook in a large saucepan with enough water to cover potatoes. Remove potatoes from pan. Peel then cut into thick slices and place in a large bowl.

1 cup canned apricots
1 cup firmly packed brown sugar
1/4 cup butter, melted
1 tsp. grated orange rind
1/4 cup chopped walnuts

Drain apricots, reserving 1/4 cup liquid. Alternate layers of potatoes, apricots and brown sugar in a greased 2 1/2 quart casserole. Combine butter, reserved apricot liquid and orange rind in a small bowl. Pour over mixture.

Bake in a 350⁰ oven for 1 hour. During the last 5 minutes of baking, sprinkle with the chopped walnuts.

SQUASH CROQUETTES

2 cups finely chopped yellow squash 1 cup finely chopped onion 1 egg, beaten 1 tsp. salt 1 tsp. pepper 1/2 cup + 1 TBSP flour	Wash squash and peel onion before chopping. Combine squash, onion, egg and seasonings. Stir in flour.

Cooking oil

Pour enough oil into a large, heavy skillet so it is 1/2" deep. Heat oil on medium-high (be careful not to over heat). Drop mixture by TBSP into the hot oil and cook until brown, turning once.
Drain on folded paper towels.

WESTERN CORN SOUFFLÉ

1 1/2 TBSP butter 4 TBSP flour 2 cups milk 1 tsp. dry mustard 1/2 tsp. salt 1 cup grated Cheddar cheese 1 cup drained canned corn	Melt butter in a medium saucepan. Stir in flour, then add milk and cook until thick, stirring to blend. Add mustard, salt and cheese. Mix in corn. Remove from heat.
1 TBSP butter 3 TBSP chopped green pepper	In a small skillet, sauté pepper in butter until limp. Add to mixture and stir.
3 eggs	Separate eggs. Beat whites until very stiff. Slightly beat yolks and add to mixture, then fold in whites.

Pour batter into a buttered 1 1/4 quart casserole that has been set in a 9" x 13" x 2" pan of hot tap water. Make sure the pan is large enough so the water does not spill over in the oven.
Bake in a 350⁰ oven for 45 minutes or until set.

ZUCCHINI FRIES

2 medium zucchini
1 egg, beaten
2 tsp. milk
1/3 cup seasoned bread crumbs
Cooking spray

Wash and scrub zucchini. Cut into halves. Cut the halves into 1/2" strips. Whisk egg and milk in a bowl until blended. Sprinkle the bread crumbs on a sheet of waxed paper. Dip each strip into the egg mixture and coat with bread crumbs.

Arrange the strips in a single layer on a baking sheet that has been sprayed with the cooking spray.
Bake in a 400⁰ oven for 8 minutes. Turn over and bake for 7 minutes longer.
Serve immediately.

CASSEROLES

ASPARAGUS CASSEROLE

3 stacks Ritz crackers
1 cup butter, melted
2 cans asparagus, drained
    (reserve juice)

Crumble crackers into a medium bowl. Add melted butter and stir together. Spray 9"x 13"x 2" pan with cooking spray and add half the cracker mix. Spread asparagus evenly over crackers.

1 can cream of mushroom soup
12 ounces grated Cheddar cheese

In a medium bowl, mix asparagus juice, soup and cheese. Mix well. Pour over asparagus. Put the rest of the cracker mixture over the top.

Bake in a 350⁰ oven for 35 minutes.

AU GRATIN POTATO CASSEROLE

1 (32 ounce) pkg. frozen
    Southern-style hash
    brown potatoes
1 (16 ounce) container sour cream
2 cups grated Cheddar cheese
1 (10 3/4 ounce) can cream of
    mushroom soup
1 small onion, finely chopped
1/4 tsp. pepper

Stir ingredients together in a large bowl.

2 cups crushed cornflakes cereal
1/4 cup butter, melted

Mix together in a small bowl and set aside.

Spoon potato mixture into a lightly greased 9"x 13"x 2" baking dish. Sprinkle cornflake mixture over the top.
Bake in a 325⁰ oven for 1 hour and 20 minutes or until bubbly.

BAKED PASTA CASSEROLE

Preheat oven to 400^0

4 cups broccoli flowerets (this is the top part of the broccoli that looks like a bunch of small flowers. Cut these off and dispose of the rest)
1 cup elbow macaroni
1 TBSP olive oil

Prepare broccoli by placing in a medium saucepan, covering with water and cook over medium-high heat until tender (about 5 mintues). Drain and rinse with cool water. Set aside. In a large saucepan, cook macaroni according to package directions. Drain and rinse with warm water. Return to pan and toss with oil. Spoon pasta into a 9" x 13" x2" casserole dish. Add broccoli.

1/4 cup butter
4 TBSP flour
1 1/2 cups milk
1/2 tsp. pepper
2 1/4 cups grated Parmesan cheese (reserve 1/4 cup for topping)
2 tsps Dijon-style mustard
1 cup diced cooked ham (you can use thick sliced ham sandwich meat)

In a medium saucepan, melt butter over medium heat, then stir in flour. Cook, stirring about 2 minutes. Whisk in milk and pepper. Stir in 2 cups cheese and mustard. Fold in ham.

1/4 cup Seasoned bread crumbs

Pour sauce over top of macaroni-broccoli mixture. Mix well. Sprinkle with bread crumbs and remaining cheese.
Bake in the preheated 400^0 oven for 25 minutes.

114

BAKED SQUASH CASSEROLE

2 pounds yellow squash
1/2 cup water

} Wash and cut into 1/2" slices. Place in a medium saucepan. Add water and cook until tender. Drain well.

3 TBSP chopped onion
3 eggs, beaten
2 cups Ritz cracker crumbs
2 tsp. parsley flakes
1/2 tsp. salt
1/4 tsp. pepper
1/2 cup butter, melted
1/2 tsp. hot sauce

} Reserve 1 cup crackers. In a large bowl, mix remaining ingredients together. Add squash and stir gently.

Spoon mixture into a lightly greased 1 1/2 quart casserole and sprinkle with remaining cracker crumbs.
Bake in a 350⁰ oven for 35 minutes.

CABBAGE ROLL CASSEROLE

Preheat oven to 350⁰

1 pound ground beef

} In a large, heavy skillet, brown meat until redness is gone. Drain well.

1/2 cup chopped onion
1/2 (29 ounce) can tomato sauce
1 3/4 pounds cabbage, chopped
1/2 cup uncooked rice
1/2 tsp. salt

} Mix all together in a large bowl. Add meat and mix well.

1 (14 ounce) can beef broth

Pour mixture into a greased 9" x 13" x 2" casserole dish. Pour broth evenly over the top. Cover with foil.
Bake in the preheated 350⁰ oven for 1 hour.
Remove cover and stir. Replace cover and cook another 30 minutes.

CHICKEN NOODLE CASSEROLE

6 ounces medium noodles } Cook until tender in a large saucepan and drain.

1 can cream of chicken soup
1 (6 ounce) can evaporated milk
1/2 tsp. salt
1 1/2 cups grated cheese
2 cups cooked, diced chicken
    (can use canned chicken)
1/4 cup chopped pimento
1 cup chopped celery
1/4 cup chopped green pepper
1 cup slivered, blanched almonds,
    toasted

} Using the same large saucepan, mix soup, milk and salt together. Heat, stirring constantly. Add cheese, chicken, pimento, celery, green pepper and half the almonds.

1 cup bread crumbs
1/4 cup butter, melted } Mix together and set aside.

Grease a 2 quart round casserole dish. Pour in the noodles and form a "nest". Pour soup mixture into the middle of the nest (it will seep into the noodles). Top with remaining almonds and the bread crumbs. Cook in a 400⁰ oven for 20 minutes.

Can't Boil Water #25: An easy way to toast almonds (or any nuts) is to place them in a heavy, ungreased skillet. Stir often over medium heat until golden brown. Or, you can follow instructions in Can't Boil Water #6.

CORN & PEA CASSEROLE

5 TBSP butter, reserve 2 TBSP
2 TBSP minced onion
1/3 cup minced celery
2 TBSP flour
2 tsp. sugar
1 tsp. salt
1/8 tsp. pepper
1/2 tsp. basil
1 1/2 cups milk

} Melt 3 TBSP butter in a heavy medium saucepan. Add onion and celery. Cook until golden. Blend in flour, sugar and seasonings. Gradually add milk, stirring constantly. Cook until thick.

2 cups whole kernel corn, drained
1 (10 ounce) box frozen peas

} Mix together in a 1 1/2 quart casserole.

1/4 cup crushed croutons
1/4 cup grated Cheddar cheese

} Melt remaining 2 TBSP butter and mix with croutons.

Pour sauce over the vegetables. Spread croutons over the top and sprinkle with cheese. Bake in a 350⁰ oven for 25 minutes.

CORN CASSEROLE

2 eggs, beaten
1/2 cup cooking oil
1 cup corn meal
1 cup milk
2 cans cream style corn
1/2 tsp. baking soda
1 tsp. garlic salt
1 medium onion, chopped
1 small can chopped green chilies
2 cups grated cheese

} In a large bowl, mix ingredients in order given.

Pour into a 9" x 13" x 2" casserole dish that has been sprayed with cooking spray. Bake in a 350⁰ oven for 1 hour.

FIVE CAN CASSEROLE

1 (10 ounce) can chicken
1 can cream mushroom soup
1 can cream chicken soup   } Mix together in a 2 quart casserole
1 can Chinese noodles   dish.
1 (5 ounce) can evaporated milk

1 cup cubed bread   } Place bread cubes in a large, heavy
2 TBSP butter, melted   skillet over medium-high heat. Stir
                                often until brown. Mix with butter.

Sprinkle bread cubes over top of mixture.
Bake in a 275⁰ oven for 30 minutes. Remove and let set before serving.

FIVE SOUP CASSEROLE

1 bell pepper, chopped   } In a large heavy skillet, sauté pepper
1 large onion, chopped   and onion in butter. Add beef and
3 TBSP butter   cook until meat is browned. Drain
3 pounds ground beef   well.

1 can cream of chicken soup
1 can cream of mushroom soup
1 can onion soup   } Combine in an extra large bowl and
1 can celery soup   stir well. Mix in meat and stir again.
1 can cheese soup
1 can Rotel tomatoes

1 medium pkg. regular size Doritoes, crushed
1 cup grated cheese

Stir Doritoes and cheese into mixture. Pour into a 8" x 13" x 3" roasting pan.
Bake in a 350⁰ oven for 45 minutes.

This dish freezes well.

FRUIT CASSEROLE

1 (1 pound, 14 ounce) can fruit
            for salad, drained
2 bananas, cut into chunks
1 cup black pitted cherries,
            drained
1/4 cup butter, melted

In a large bowl, mix the fruits together. Pour butter over the fruit.

1/2 cup brown sugar
2 TBSP cornstarch
1 TBSP mild curry powder

Mix together in a small bowl and pour over fruit. Mix lightly.

1 cup heavy cream, whipped

Pour into a buttered 1 1/2 quart casserole.
Bake in a 350⁰ oven for 40 minutes.
Serve warm with whipped cream.

GRITS CASSEROLE

4 cups water
1 cup quick cooking grits
1 tsp. salt

Cook grits in a large saucepan according to time on package.

2 cups grated sharp cheddar
            cheese
1/4 cup butter, melted
1 can chopped green chilies
2 TBSP chopped pimento
2 eggs, beaten

Combine everything with the cooked grits.

Pour into a greased 9" x 13" x 2" casserole dish.
Bake in a 350⁰ oven for 45 minutes.

ITALIAN GREEN BEAN CASSEROLE

1 (10 3/4 ounce) can cream of
        mushroom soup
1/2 cup milk
1 1/2 tsp. soy sauce
1/4 tsp. pepper
2 (14 1/2 ounce) cans Italian
        green beans, drained
1 1/3 cups French fried onions,
        divided

Reserve half the onion rings. Mix remaining ingredients together in a 1 1/2 quart casserole dish.

Bake in a 350⁰ oven for 25 minutes. Stir, then sprinkle remaining onions on top. Bake 10 minutes until onions are golden in color.

ORIENTAL CASSEROLE

2 cups sliced celery (1" pieces)
1/2 tsp. salt
1/2 cup water

In a large saucepan, cook celery with salt in the water until tender. This will take about 8 minutes. Drain. Return to saucepan.

1 can peas, drained
1 can sliced water chestnuts,
        drained
1 can cream of chicken soup
1/4 cup diced pimentos
1/4 cup slivered almonds

Mix together with the celery.

1/2 cup soft bread crumbs
2 TBSP butter, melted

Combine in a small bowl and set aside.

Pour mixture into a 1 1/2 quart casserole dish and sprinkle with the bread crumbs.
Bake in a 350⁰ oven for 35 minutes.

SPINACH CASSEROLE

3 pkgs. chopped, frozen spinach

} In a medium saucepan, cook spinach according to package directions. Pour into a large strainer and let drain for at least 1 hour.

8 ounces Velveeta cheese
8 ounces sharp cheese, grated
1 pint sour cream
1 small onion, chopped

} Mix together in a large bowl, add the spinach and mix well.

1 cup seasoned croutons
1/2 cup grated Parmesan cheese

Pour mixture into a buttered 2 quart casserole dish. Top with croutons then sprinkle cheese over the croutons. Cover with foil.
Bake in a 350^0 oven for 30 minutes.

SWEET POTATO CASSEROLE

3 cups cooked, mashed
            sweet potatoes
1/2 cup butter
3/4 cup sugar

} Mix well in a 1 1/2 quart casserole dish.

1 cup packed brown sugar
5 TBSP butter
1/3 cup flour
1/2 cup chopped pecans

} Melt butter and add remaining ingredients. Cool and crumble on top of potato mixture.

Bake in a 350^0 oven for 30 minutes.

NOTE: canned sweet potatoes may be used. Drain and then place into a medium bowl and mash well.

TUNA CASSEROLE
with
LEMON MUSTARD SAUCE

1 (10 1/4 ounce) can cream of
        potato soup
1/2 cup water
2 (6 to 7 ounce each) cans tuna,
        drained & flaked
1 tsp. grated lemon peel
2 TBSP lemon juice   In a large bowl, thoroughly mix
1/2 cup finely chopped celery   together in order given.
1/4 cup finely chopped onion
1 TBSP snipped fresh parsley
1/8 tsp. pepper
3 eggs, beaten
3 slices dry bread, finely crumbled

Pour into well buttered 1 1/2 quart casserole.
Bake, uncovered, in a 350⁰ oven for 60 minutes.
Serve with lemon mustard sauce.

LEMON MUSTARD SAUCE

2 TBSP butter   In a heavy saucepan at medium
2 TBSP flour   heat, melt butter. Blend in flour,
1/2 tsp. salt   salt and pepper to form a smooth
1/8 tsp. pepper   paste. Gradually add hot water
1 cup hot water   and mustard, stirring until smooth.
1 tsp. prepared mustard   Bring to a boil and cook for 2
1 tsp. grated lemon peel   minutes. Stir in lemon peel and
1 TBSP lemon juice   juice.

1/2 cup mayonnaise

Just before serving the casserole, fold mayonnaise into the sauce. Spoon over
tuna.

VEGETABLE CASSEROLE

1 pkg. frozen cauliflower
1 pkg. frozen tiny green peas
} Prepare according to package directions. Drain, mix and divide in half.

1/2 pint sour cream
8 ounces grated cheese
2 TBSP butter, melted
1/2 tsp. salt
1/4 tsp. pepper
} Mix together in a medium bowl and set aside.

Layer half the vegetables in bottom of a 2 quart casserole dish. Spread half the cheese mixture over top. Repeat, using remaining ingredients.
Bake in a 325⁰ oven for 15 minutes or until cheese is melted and bubbly.

WALL'S BROCCOLI CASSEROLE

1 pkg. frozen chopped broccoli
1/2 can cream of mushroom soup
1/2 cup grated sharp cheddar
       cheese
1 egg, well beaten
1/2 cup mayonnaise
1 TBSP grated onion
1/2 tsp. salt
1/4 tsp. pepper
} Cook broccoli 5 minutes in a medium saucepan using 1/2 cup of water. Drain well. Return to pan. Combine remaining ingredients with broccoli. Stir well. Pour into a greased 2 quart casserole dish.

1/2 cup cheese crackers, crumbled

Sprinkle cracker crumbs over mixture.
Bake in a 400⁰ oven for 30 minutes.

NOTE: Do Not substitute salad dressing for mayonnaise.
       May be refrigerated or frozen before baking.

WHAT THE DICKENS?
Sweet Potato Crunch

2 (30 ounce) cans mashed sweet
        potatoes, drained
1 3/4 cups sugar
1 cup milk
1/2 cup butter, melted
4 eggs, lightly beaten
1 tsp. salt
1 tsp. cinnamon
1 tsp. vanilla extract

In a large bowl, combine and mix well. Spoon into a greased 9" x 13" x 2" baking dish.

2 cups chopped pecans
2 cups brown sugar
2/3 cup flour
6 TBSP butter, melted

Mix first 3 ingredients in a medium bowl. Stir in butter. Sprinkle over top of potato mixture.

Bake in a 350⁰ oven for 35 minutes.

MAIN DISHES

Spice & Herbs
General Guideline

* When first experimenting, easy does it! Use just enough to heighten natural food flavors.

* Start with 1/4 tsp. dried herbs per four servings; or per 1 pound of meat, poultry, fish; or per 2 cups sauce, vegetables, soup.

* Measure dried herbs, then crush in palm of hand before adding to items to be cooked. Crushing the herbs helps hasten to release their flavors.

* If substituting fresh herbs for dried, use 3 to 4 times as much.

* Add herbs at the same time as salt and pepper to meats, vegetables, sauces and soups.

* In long-cooking foods, such as stews, add herbs during last half hour of cooking time.

* Add herbs to juices or cold sauces well ahead of time. Let stand overnight if possible.

* Balance the seasonings. One strongly seasoned dish per meal is generally a good rule.

BBQ HAMBURGER MIX

This makes a very large amount.

4 medium onions, chopped 3 cloves garlic, finely chopped 2 cups chopped celery with tops 1/2 cup shortening	In a large heavy pot, heat shortening on medium-high heat. Add remaining ingredients and cook until onions are a clear color.
4 pounds ground beef 4 tsp. salt 1/2 tsp. pepper 3 TBSP Worcestershire sauce 2 (12 ounce) bottles ketchup	Add beef to onion mixture and cook until redness disappears from meat stirring often. Drain well. Add remaining ingredients. Simmer 20 minutes, stirring often.

Cool mixture quickly by sitting pan in the sink filled with 3" to 4" of cold water. To freeze mixture that is not used immediately: Spoon mixture into 5 one pint freezer containers. Seal and label with name and date (do not use a marks-a-lot, to label plastic containers, it bleeds through the plastic. Use a sharpie.) It is best not to stack the containers until thoroughly frozen. The mixture may be stored in freezer up to 3 months.

This is a great recipe to use for BBQ sandwiches or chili dogs. Add some to cooked noodles or make a "mock pizza" by spooning mix over a lightly toasted English muffin then topping with grated cheese.
Use your imagination.

BEEF STROGANOFF

2 pounds chuck steak
1 cup flour
1/4 cup cooking oil
1 cup tomato juice
1 cup water
1 1/2 tsp. salt
1/4 tsp. pepper

Trim excess fat from meat. Cut meat into thin 1" strips and roll in flour. Discard leftover flour. Heat oil in a large, heavy skillet on medium-high heat. Brown meat, turning often. Remove excess fat from skillet using a spoon. Add tomato juice, water, salt and pepper. Cook, covered, over low heat until tender (20 to 30 minutes). Stir occasionally.

1/4 cup cooking oil
2 cups sliced onions
1/4 pound mushrooms, sliced

Using a medium sized skillet, brown onions and mushrooms over medium heat. Transfer to meat mixture using a slotted spoon. Cover and simmer.

6 cups cooked noodles (use directions on package to cook noodles)
1 cup sour cream

Mix sour cream into noodles.
To serve, place noodles in a large, shallow bowl and top with beef mixture.
Serve immediately.

BEER CAN GRILLED CHICKEN

1 (4 to 5 pound) roasting chicken
3 TBSP dry spice rub, divided
1 TBSP cooking oil

Remove neck and giblets from chicken (found in cavity of the chicken) and discard, then rinse well inside and out. Pat dry with paper towels. Coat chicken with cooking oil and rub half the dry spice mix over the chicken.

1 (12 ounce) can of beer

Open beer can, pour out about 1/4 cup of beer, then make an extra hole in the top of the can with a can opener. Sprinkle remaining dry rub mixture inside the beer can. Holding the chicken with the opening of the body cavity at the bottom (chicken legs are down), lower the chicken onto the beer can so the can fits into the cavity. of the chicken. Pull the legs forward to form a sort of tripod so the bird stands upright (the rear leg of the tripod is the beer can). Tuck the wing tips behind the chickens back.

Place the chicken-beer can on the hot grill. The chicken will appear to be sitting on the grill. Cook chicken away from the direct heat for 1 1/4 to 1 1/2 hours. Remove from can and let rest on a platter for 10 minutes. NOTE: Be careful not to spill contents of can when removing the chicken because it will be very hot.

A metal 'holder' that will hold the can and chicken can be purchased at most any store that sells outdoor utensils. It keeps the can and chicken from toppling over on the grill.

Can't Boil Water #26: To test if chicken is done, pierce one side of the breast with a sharp fork, then the thigh. The fork should go into the meat easily.

BURGER-SQUASH QUICHE

1 purchased uncooked
          pie crust dough

Set unwrapped dough on the cabinet top to warm, then unroll and put in a 9" deep dish pie pan, following directions in Can't Boil Water #21.

3/4 pound ground beef
1/2 tsp. garlic salt

In a large, heavy skillet combine and brown. Drain and set aside.

2 medium squash, washed &
          sliced thin
1/2 medium onion, peeled &
          sliced thin
3 TBSP butter

Melt butter in the same skillet that you browned the meat in on medium-high heat and cook squash and onion until wilted.

5 eggs, beaten
1/2 cup mayonnaise
1/2 cup half & half
2 cups grated cheese blend
1/2 tsp. salt
1/4 tsp. pepper

Mix in a large bowl and stir well. Add meat and stir again.

Place squash-onion mixture on top of crust. Add meat mixture.
Bake in a 350⁰ oven for 45 minutes.

CHEESEBURGER MINI MEATLOAF'S
ACK's original

1 1/2 pounds ground beef
1 TBSP bacon bits
1/2 cup chopped onion
1/2 cup ketchup
1 egg, beaten
3/4 cup seasoned bread crumbs
8 crushed crackers
1/8 tsp. garlic powder
1/2 tsp. cumin or chili powder

In a large bowl, break up ground beef then add remaining ingredients. Combine well.

6 slices American cheese

Shape meat mixture into 6 oval loaves. Cut each in half lengthwise, then place 1 slice of cheese, folded in half, on the bottom half of the loaf. Replace top and squish together pinching seam together. Reshape.
Spray a 9" x 13" x 2" pan with cooking spray. Place mini's in pan.
Cook in a 350⁰ oven for 30 minutes.

CHICKEN CHOW MEIN

2 TBSP cornstarch
1/4 cup water

Mix together, stirring until cornstarch is dissolved.

2 cups chicken broth
2 cups chopped celery
1 small onion, sliced
1/2 tsp. salt
2 TBSP soy sauce
2 cups bean sprouts, drained
      or mixed Chinese vegetables
2 cups finely chopped, cooked
          chicken

Cook celery and onion in chicken broth 20 minutes. Add remaining ingredients, including cornstarch mixture.

Cook 10 minutes, stirring constantly.
Serve on cooked rice or crisp noodles.

CHICKEN with STUFFING

1 pkg. cornbread stuffing mix
4 cups cooked chicken, cut into
    small pieces
1/2 cup butter
1/2 cup flour
1/4 tsp. salt
Dash pepper
4 cups canned chicken broth
6 eggs, slightly beaten in a small
    bowl

Prepare stuffing according to directions on package. Spread in a 9" x 13" x 2" dish. Top with a layer of chicken. Melt butter in a medium saucepan. Blend in flour and seasonings, making a paste. Add broth and stir over heat until thickened. Stir small amount of hot mixture into eggs and pour it back into the saucepan. Stir until blended and then pour over the stuffing and chicken in the dish.

Bake in a 325^0 oven for 45 minutes or until a knife comes out clean. Let stand 5 minutes, then cut into squares. Serve topped with sauce.

SAUCE:
    1 cup cream of mushroom soup
    1 cup sour cream
    1/4 cup milk
    1/4 cup chopped pimento

Blend soup, milk and sour cream in a medium saucepan. Heat through. Remove from heat. Add pimento and stir.
Serve over chicken squares.

Can't Boil Water #27: Cook chicken with ease. In a large heavy pot, bring 4 cups water to a boil. Add 1 tsp. salt, 1 stalk celery and 1/2 onion sliced thick. Gently slide four to six individually quick-frozen chicken breast pieces into the water. Bring water back to a boil. Cover pot tightly, turn off heat and let stand 30 minutes. Drain chicken breasts, discarding celery and onion. Place in a bowl, cover and refrigerate to cool completely.

CHICKEN SPAGHETTI

2 (16 ounce) boxes spaghetti
1 TBSP olive oil
1 tsp. salt

Fill an extra large pot 3/4 full with water. Add olive oil and salt. Bring to a boil. Break spaghetti in half and drop in small bunches into the boiling water. Stir, then bring water back to a boil. Cover pot with a tight fitting lid. Remove pot from heat and let sit for 20 minutes. Pour spaghetti into a large strainer and rinse with very warm water. Spray pot with cooking spray and pour spaghetti back into the pot. Cover to keep warm.

3 TBSP butter
2 large buttons garlic, sliced thin
1 large onion, sliced thin
4 (10 ounce) cans chicken
2 (14.5 ounce) cans
    dices tomatoes
2 cans cream of mushroom soup
1/2 tsp. salt
1/4 tsp. pepper

Melt butter in a medium skillet. Add garlic and onion. Cook on medium-high heat until onions are a clear color. Drain chicken and break into small chunks. Place everything in the pot with the spaghetti. Stir well.

Set the pot of chicken spaghetti over a large skillet or pan of simmering water. The skillet (or pan) should fit the bottom of the pot snuggly as if the two were a very large double boiler. Let set, stirring occasionally, 3 to 4 hours to mix flavors. Check the water in the bottom skillet (or pan) occasionally to be sure it stays at a 1" to 2" level. Refrigerate left overs.
Makes a very large amount.

CHILI-TAMALE BAKE

2 (15 ounce) cans chili without
    beans
1 (15 ounce) can pinto beans,
    drained
1 (15 ounce) can tamales

Pour chili and beans into a 1 1/2
quart baking dish.
Remove wrappers from tamales and
arrange on top.

1/2 cup grated Parmesan cheese

Bake in a 375⁰ oven for 30 minutes.
Sprinkle cheese over the top and serve immediately.

CHUCK WAGON CHILI

4 pounds ground beef

In a large heavy skillet, cook in
batches on medium-high heat
stirring until meat crumbles and
is no longer pink. Drain in a large
strainer and place into a 6 quart
slow cooker.

2 medium onions, chopped
1 green pepper, chopped
2 garlic cloves, minced
3 (14 1/2 ounce) cans diced
        tomatoes, undrained
1 (6 ounce) can tomato paste
1/4 cup chili powder
1 TBSP sugar
1 tsp. salt
1 tsp. pepper
1/2 tsp. ground red pepper
2 (16 ounce) cans pinto beans,
    drained

Stir all ingredients into meat
mixture. Cook, covered, on high 5
to 6 hours.

Can be frozen in ziploc bags up to 1 month.

CHUCK WAGON SKILLET

1 1/2 pounds ground beef 1 medium onion, chopped 1 tsp. salt 1/4 tsp. pepper	In a large heavy skillet, brown meat and onions on medium-high heat. Drain, then return to skillet and add salt and pepper.
8 ounces cubed cheddar cheese 1/2 cup chopped celery 1/2 cup chopped ripe olives 2 cups medium noodles, uncooked 1 (16 ounce) can stewed tomatoes 1/2 cup water	In layers, add cheese, celery, olives and noodles to the meat mixture. Pour on tomatoes and water.

Cover and heat on medium until steam begins to escape from under the lid. When it starts to steam, turn to low and simmer for 35 minutes. Do not remove cover.

CRÊPE BURRITOS

1 pound ground beef 1/2 green bell pepper 1 onion, chopped 1/2 cup water 1/2 cup canned refried beans 1 (1.5 ounce) pkg. taco seasoning mix (reserve 3 TBSP)	In a large heavy skillet, cook meat and drain. Return to skillet and add green pepper, onion, water and taco mix (remember to save 3 TBSP). Cook mixture until thick, stirring frequently. Add beans and set aside.
1 cup baking mix 1 cup milk 2 eggs, slightly beaten	Combine baking mix and the reserved 3 TBSP taco mix. Mix together milk and eggs in a small bowl and add to dry mixture. Whisk until smooth.

Heat an 8" non-stick skillet. Pour 1/4 cup batter into hot skillet and immediately tilt skillet counter-clockwise around to distribute batter into a very large, thin pancake. Cook until golden (about 2 minutes), turn and brown the other side. Keep crêpes stacked between wax paper until ready to assemble with meat mixture..
Divide meat mixture evenly on crêpes. Roll crêpes, tucking ends in and place seam side down on a well greased, large cookie sheet.
Cook in a 375⁰ oven for 10 minutes.
GARNISH: lettuce, tomato, grated cheese, sour cream, ripe olives, hot salsa.

CROCK-POT BBQ BEEF

2 pounds ground beef
      or 2 pounds left-over roast
      chopped into small pieces
1/4 cup brown sugar
1/2 tsp. pepper
1 medium onion, chopped
1 cup tomato sauce
3 TBSP Worcestershire sauce
3 TBSP molasses
3 TBSP cider vinegar
1 TBSP chili powder
1 tsp. garlic salt
1 tsp. dry mustard
1/2 tsp. salt

If using ground beef, cook in a large heavy skillet until brown, then drain.

Add meat and remaining ingredients to a 6 quart crock pot, cover, and cook for 5 hours. Serve over buns or rolls.

GARDEN TUNA SPAGHETTI

1 (16 ounce) pkg. spaghetti
2 tsp. olive oil
1/2 tsp. salt

Fill a extra large pot 3/4 full with water. Add olive oil and salt. Bring to a boil. Break spaghetti in half and drop in small bunches into the boiling water. Stir, then bring water back to a boil. Cover pot with a tight fitting lid. Remove pot from heat and let sit for 20 minutes. Pour spaghetti into a large strainer and rinse with very warm water. Spray pot with cooking spray and pour spaghetti back into the pot. Cover to keep warm.

1 can cream of celery soup
1 cup milk
1/2 tsp. onion salt
1 (13 ounce) can tuna in water, drained
1 (4 ounce) jar diced pimentos
2 cups grated Cheddar cheese
1 avocado, peeled and cubed

Pour soup into a medium saucepan. Gradually add milk stirring to combine. Add salt, tuna and pimento. Heat on low 15 minutes. Add cheese and stir until the cheese is melted. Add avocado.

Serve tuna sauce over spaghetti in individual bowls.

GLAZED BAKED HAM

4 pound canned ham
Whole cloves
1 cup honey

Place ham, fat side up, on a rack in a shallow baking pan. Push cloves, stem side down, into top of ham about every 2" over the top. Drizzle with 1/2 cup honey.

Bake in a 325⁰ oven, drizzling more honey over the top of the ham every 15 minutes. Bake for a total of 45 minutes.

GREAT BBQ SAUCE

16 ounces tomato sauce
1 TBSP brown sugar
1 TBSP apple cider vinegar
1 tsp. chili powder
1 tsp. Worcestershire sauce
6 ounces Coca Cola, regular or
              diet
1/2 tsp. salt
1/4 tsp. pepper
1/4 tsp. garlic powder

Combine all ingredients in a medium saucepan.

Cook, stirring occasionally, over low heat until blended. Do not boil.

HOT MEAT SANDWICH

Sliced cooked beef, pork, chicken
or turkey
6 hoagie buns or burger buns
1 (10.5 ounce) can gravy
(beef or chicken according
to meat used)

Heat gravy at medium heat in a
medium saucepan. Add sliced meat
and simmer until heated through.

Spread buns with soft butter and toast using the oven broiler. Top with meat,
adding a good scoop of gravy.

IMPOSSIBLE TACO PIE

Preheat oven to 400⁰. Grease a 9" deep dish pie plate.

1 pound ground beef
1/2 cup chopped onion
1 pkg. taco seasoning mix
1 (4 ounce) can chopped green
chilies, drained

In a large heavy skillet, cook and stir
beef and onion over medium heat
until brown. Drain well. Return
meat to skillet. Stir in seasoning
mix. Spread in the pie plate and
sprinkle with chilies.

3/4 cup baking mix
3 eggs, beaten
1 1/4 cups milk

Beat together in a medium bowl
until smooth. Pour over meat
mixture.

2 tomatoes, sliced & placed on folded paper towels to drain
1 cup grated Monterey Jack cheese

Reserve tomatoes and cheese.
Bake in the 400⁰ pre-heated oven for 25 minutes.
Top with the tomatoes and sprinkle with cheese.
Bake 8 minutes longer or until knife inserted between center and edge comes
out clean. Remove from oven and let cool for 5 minutes before slicing.
Serve with sour cream and shredded lettuce, if desired.

IRISH STEW with DUMPLINGS

2 cans stew
1 can regular biscuits
} Heat stew in a large saucepan until bubbling hot. Cut biscuits into fourths, place on top of stew and cover with saucepan lid.

Simmer 15 minutes without lifting lid.

LIP SMACKING BBQ RIBS

Start a fire in the smoker. Let heat get to 225^0.
Place 2 to 3 sides (stacked) of pork ribs in the smoker.
Do not place directly above fire.
Cook 5 hours at 225^0
Rotate ribs approximately every hour.
After 5 hours, remove ribs from smoker, wrap in heavy foil and place
in a preheated oven at 225^0 for 2 hours.
Cut heat to 200^0 and leave in the oven for 2 additional hours.
Remove ribs from oven, leaving in foil, place in brown bags, folded tightly and let set for one hour.
BROWN BAG IS VERY IMPORTANT.
Putting a BBQ rub on the ribs 2 hours before cooking or the night before also helps.

Try the "Great BBQ Sauce" recipe on page 138 with these cooked ribs.

LUNCH MEAT and BEAN COMBO

2 cans pork n' beans
1/4 cup ketchup
1 TBSP prepared mustard
1/2 tsp. Worcestershire sauce

} Mix together and pour into a 1 1/2 quart baking dish.

2 cans lunch meat

} Slice lunch meat in half lengthwise. Score 1 side of each half into 7 sections, leaving the sections in tact (do not cut completely through the lunch meat). Arrange on top of beans.

Bake in a 375⁰ oven for 25 minutes.

Bake in a 375^0 oven for 25 minutes.

MAIN DISH STEAMED CABBAGE

1 bottle beer, open & let set at room temperature until flat.

2 pork chops
1/3 pound ground beef
1 medium onion, finely chopped
1/2 cup water

} Cut pork chops into bite size pieces. In a large, deep skillet or dutch oven, brown meats. Add onion and sauté until clear. Add water and de-grease bottom of skillet by scraping with a spatula.

1 medium-large cabbage
1 cup corn relish
1/4 tsp. onion salt
1/4 tsp. garlic salt
5 drops Magi seasoning

} Cut cabbage into quarters and add to meat mixture. Add remaining ingredients. Add the beer.

Cook 20 to 30 minutes, covered to keep in moisture.

Can't Boil Water #28: Magi seasoning, steak sauce and Worcestershire sauce are interchangeable.

MEAL in a POT

1/4 cup flour
1 tsp. paprika
3/4 tsp. salt
1/8 tsp. pepper
4 chicken thighs or legs
3 TBSP shortening

Place dry ingredients into a 1 quart ziploc bag. Zip bag and shake to mix. Drop the chicken into the bag, zip and shake to coat meat. Heat shortening in a large heavy skillet on medium-high heat. Brown chicken on all sides, then reduce heat.

1/4 cup water
2 TBSP butter
2 carrots, scraped & cut in large pieces
1/2 pound green beans, washed
2 medium potatoes, peeled and quartered
2 large apples, quartered
4 TBSP sugar
1/2 tsp. cinnamon

Add water and butter, then vegetables to chicken. Arrange apples on top. Mix sugar and cinnamon, then sprinkle on top of apples.

Cover and cook on low 45 minutes to 1 hour or until meat is tender.

MEXICAN PIE

Preheat oven to 450⁰.

1 pound ground lean pork
1 large onion, sliced
1 (16 ounce) can tomato sauce
1/2 cup ketchup
1 (12 ounce) can whole kernel
        corn, drained
2 TBSP chili powder
1 tsp. salt
1/4 tsp. pepper
1 tsp. cumin
1 tsp. garlic powder

In a large heavy skillet, cook meat and onion until meat is brown and onion is tender. Drain off fat. Stir in remaining ingredients and heat to boiling. Reduce heat and simmer 10 minutes.

While meat mixture is simmering, prepare pastry.
Measure dry ingredients into a medium bowl. Cut in shortening with a pastry blender until mixture resembles coarse meal. Sprinkle with water until flour is moistened. Roll dough on a lightly floured pastry cloth the size of the top of a two quart baking dish.

CORNMEAL PASTRY
1 cup flour
1/4 cup yellow cornmeal
1/2 tsp. salt
1/3 cup + 1 TBSP shortening
3 TBSP cold water

Pour meat mixture into the baking dish. Cover with the pastry. Seal edges of pastry to the baking dish.
Bake in a 400⁰ pre-heated oven for 35 minutes.

MOCK ENCHILADAS

2 cups grated taco blend cheese
2 cups minced onions
4 cups corn chips

} Butter a 7 1/2" x 12" x 2" baking dish. Reserve 1/2 cup cheese. Alternately add cheese, onions and corn chips in layers into the baking dish.

1 large can chili without beans

} Pour chili into a medium saucepan and heat. It does not need to boil.

Pour chili over ingredients in baking dish. Sprinkle remaining cheese over top. Bake in a 350⁰ for 20 minutes or until cheese has melted.

PAN PIZZA

Preheat oven to 375⁰.

1/2 pound ground beef
1/4 tsp. salt
1/4 tsp. pepper
1 small onion
1/2 green bell pepper, seeds
        removed

} Chop the onion and bell pepper. Place all ingredients into a large heavy skillet and cook on medium-high heat stirring until beef is browned and crumbly. Drain in a large strainer.

1 (10 ounce) pkg. refrigerated
        pizza dough
1 (16 ounce) jar seasoned tomato
        sauce
3 ounces sliced pepperoni
3/4 cup grated mozzarella cheese

} Press the dough into a greased 8" deep-dish pie pan. Trim excess dough leaving 1" of the dough over the edge of the dish. Turn the edges of the dough under and flute edges. Spread tomato sauce over the dough. Sprinkle beef mixture evenly over the sauce. Arrange pepperoni slices evenly over the top of the meat. Sprinkle cheese evenly over the pepperoni.

Bake in a pre-heated 375⁰ oven for 25 minutes or until cheese is bubbly and crust is golden brown.

PATIO SUPPER

1 green pepper, seeds removed
2 pounds ground beef
1 small onion, chopped

Chop the green pepper. In a large heavy skillet, stir together all ingredients and cook until beef is brown. Drain in a large strainer and return to skillet.

1/4 tsp. garlic powder
1 cup ripe olives, pitted, including
          1/4 cup olive liquid
1/4 pound cubed Cheddar cheese
1/4 tsp. pepper
1 (16 ounce) can diced tomatoes
1/4 tsp. salt
1 (8 ounce) pkg. noodles,
          uncooked

Add all ingredients to meat mixture. Cover and reduce heat to simmer.

Cook about 20 minutes or until noodles are tender, stirring occasionally.

PIZZA PIE

1 1/2 pounds pork sausage

In a large heavy skillet, cook sausage until brown, stirring occasionally. Drain very well.

6 hamburger buns, split &
          buttered
1 cup tomato paste
1/2 pound grated sharp cheese
2 tsp. oregano

Toast buns under oven broiler at 400^0 until golden brown.

Spread 1 TBSP tomato paste on each bun half. Sprinkle 2 TBSP cheese and 1/8 tsp. oregano on each bun half. Top with sausage and remaining cheese.

RANCH BBQ MUFFINS

1 pound ground beef
1/2 cup ketchup
3 TBSP brown sugar
1 TBSP cider vinegar
1/2 tsp. chili powder

In a large heavy skillet brown beef. Drain in a large strainer and return to skillet.
In a small bowl, stir remaining ingredients together, then add to meat and stir well. Remove from heat.

1 (10 ounce) pkg. canned biscuits
1 (12 cup) muffin pan

Separate dough into 10 biscuits. Flatten into 5" circles. Press each biscuit into the inside of the bottom and up the sides of a muffin cup until all are filled.

1 cup grated cheddar cheese

Divide meat mixture into the muffin cups, using about 1/4 cup for each.
Sprinkle cheese on top.
Bake in a 375⁰ oven for 20 minutes or until golden brown.
Remove the pan from oven and let cool for 5 minutes, then remove the muffin from the muffin cups.

NOTE: When using a muffin pan and all of the muffin cups are filled except one or two, fill the empty cup (s) 1/4 full with water. This keeps them from burning while the rest of the filled cups cook.

SALAMI TREAT

8 slices rye bread with
    caraway seed
Soft butter
16 slices small salami
   (about 1 pound)
8 thin slices onion
4 (1" thick) slices cream cheese
1/2 cup hamburger relish

Spread both sides of bread with the soft butter. Place 2 salami slices on bread. Cover with onion slices and a slice of cream cheese. Top with 2 more salami slices. Spread relish over salami. Top with remaining bread slices.

Place sandwiches on a griddle or grill and brown lightly on both sides.

SALMON ALASKA

1 (16 ounce) can pink salmon
1/4 cup dill pickles, chopped

Place salmon in a strainer to drain. Remove skin and bones from the salmon, then discard. Flake the salmon with a fork in a medium bowl and toss with pickles.

1 cup mayonnaise
2 TBSP lemon juice
1 1/2 tsp. parsley flakes
Dash cayenne pepper

In a small bowl, combine and set aside.

2 egg whites (to separate eggs,
    see page 18)

Beat until stiff but not dry. Fold into mayonnaise mixture.

6 tomato slices
6 slices white or wheat bread, toasted

Place a tomato slice on each piece of toast. Cover with salmon. Spoon mayonnaise mixture over each sandwich.
Broil about 12" from broiler 6 to 8 minutes or until lightly browned.

SALMON QUESADILLAS

1 (16 ounce) can pink salmon
8 ounces grated Mexican 3 cheese blend

} Place salmon in a strainer to drain. Remove skin and bones from the salmon, then discard. In a medium bowl flake salmon with a fork then combine with cheese.

4 (10") burrito sized flour tortillas
1 can whole green chilies, cut into strips
4 TBSP butter

Divide salmon mixture evenly over center of tortillas. Divide chili strips and place over salmon mixture.
Fold each tortilla in half.
In a large heavy skillet, melt 1 TBSP butter and spread evenly over bottom.
Heat to medium-high and fry tortilla until golden brown. Turn and brown on second side.
Cut in half and serve hot with garnishes.

GARNISHES: Sour cream, salsa or guacamole.

SKILLET CORNED BEEF and CABBAGE

1 (12 ounce) can corned beef
2 TBSP butter

} Brown beef with butter in a large heavy skillet, breaking up meat with a fork.

1 medium size cabbage
1 tsp. salt
Dash pepper

} Wash, core and coarsely chop the cabbage. Add to corned beef then add salt and pepper. Toss lightly.

Simmer tightly covered for 10 minutes or until cabbage is fork tender, stirring often.

SOUR CREAM ENCHILADAS

2 pounds ground beef
1 pkg. taco seasoning mix
1 (4.5 ounce) can chopped green
    chilies, divided

Brown meat in a large skillet, stirring until crumbled and brown. Drain well. Stir in taco seasoning mix and half of the chopped chilies. Set aside.

1 can cream of chicken soup
1 can cream of mushroom soup
1 (8 ounce) container sour cream

Using remaining chilies, stir together with soups and sour cream in a medium bowl.

8 (8") flour tortillas
2 cups grated Mexican cheese blend

Pour half the soup mixture into a lightly greased 9" x 13" x 2" baking dish.
Spoon beef mixture evenly down centers of tortillas and roll up. Place, seam side down, over soup mixture in the baking dish.
Top evenly with remaining soup mixture and sprinkle top with cheese.
Bake in a 350⁰ oven for 25 minutes or until heated through.

SPAGHETTI & MEATBALLS

2 cans spaghetti in tomato sauce
1 can meatballs with gravy

In a large saucepan, combine ingredients and simmer, covered, 10 minutes or until thoroughly heated. Stir carefully to prevent meatballs from coming apart.

1/2 cup Parmesan cheese

Spoon mixture into bowls and sprinkle with cheese.
Serve hot.

SPAGHETTI *with* MEAT SAUCE

2 cups BBQ hamburger mix
   (recipe on page 127)   }   Heat in a medium saucepan. Do
Dash cayenne pepper   not boil.
1/4 tsp. garlic salt

6 ounces spaghetti   }   In a large saucepan filled 3/4 full
with water, add olive oil and salt. Bring to a boil and add spaghetti. Bring to boil again, cover pot, remove from heat and let set for 20 minutes. Drain in a large strainer. Spray saucepan with cooking spray and return spaghetti to pan. Cover until ready to serve.

1/2 cup grated Parmesan cheese

Serve hot sauce over spaghetti and top with grated cheese.

SPANISH RICE *with* VIENNA SAUSAGE

2 (15 ounce) cans Spanish rice   }   Spread rice in a 9" pie pan. Arrange
2 (4 ounce) cans Vienna sausages   Vienna sausages over the top and
1/2 cup grated taco cheese   sprinkle with cheese.

Bake in a 375⁰ oven for 20 minutes.

SWISS STEAK with RICE

2 pounds round steak, 1" thick
2 tsp. salt
1/2 cup pepper
3 TBSP flour
3 TBSP shortening

Cut meat in 1" strips. Place salt, pepper and flour in a 1 quart ziploc bag and shake. Add steak and shake. Heat shortening in a large heavy skillet and brown meat on both sides.

1 medium onion, thinly sliced
1 cup uncooked rice
1 can tomato soup
1/2 cup water
1 1/2 cups tomato juice

Add all ingredients to skillet with meat. Turn heat to medium-low, cover skillet.

Cook 30 to 45 minutes or until meat is tender and rice is fluffy.

TUNA with MUSHROOM SAUCE on TOAST

1 (7 ounce) can tuna in water,
            drained
1 can cream of mushroom soup,
            undiluted

In a medium saucepan, heat tuna and soup. Do not boil.

4 slices buttered toast

Place toast on plates and top with tuna mixture.
Serve hot.

VEGGIE-BURGER PIZZA

1 pound ground beef
1 medium onion, sliced thin
2 medium yellow squash,
    sliced thin
2 TBSP olive oil

} Cook meat in a large heavy skillet. Drain well. Using same skillet, sauté vegetables with olive oil.

2 tomatoes, sliced thin & placed on paper towels to drain
Easy pizza sauce (recipe below)
2 cups grated Italian cheese
Pizza dough, recipe on page 89 (or purchase crust already prepared, your choice)

If using dough, work onto a 14" round pizza pan. Bake in a 425⁰ oven for 10 minutes.
Spread sauce over crust and layer with meat, vegetables and tomato slices.
Sprinkle with cheese.
Bake 12 to 17 minutes or until heated through and cheese melts.

VERY EASY PIZZA SAUCE

2 TBSP olive oil
1 TBSP minced fresh garlic
1/4 cup finely chopped onion
1 tsp. dried oregano
1 tsp. dried basil
1/2 tsp. salt
1/4 tsp. pepper

} In a medium saucepan, sauté garlic and onions in olive oil until tender. Add remaining ingredients and continue cooking a few more minutes.

1 (15 ounce) can tomato sauce
3 TBSP tomato paste

Add sauce and paste to pan. Simmer on low heat for 10 minutes.
Makes about 1 1/2 cups.

DESSERTS
CAKES
PIES
COOKIES & CANDY

CAKES

MIXTURE TO GREASE PANS

1 1/4 cups shortening
1 1/4 cups flour
1/4 cup cooking oil

} Mix all ingredients with an electric mixer until creamy.

Place in a jar that has a screw on lid and keep tightly covered in the refrigerator.

Can't Boil Water #29: The above recipe can be used for any recipe that calls for greasing and flouring a pan.

7 UP CAKE

1 cup butter
1/2 cup shortening
3 cups sugar
} Cream together in a large bowl with an electric mixer until smooth and fluffy.

5 eggs
1 1/2 tsp. vanilla
3 cups flour
1 (7 ounce) bottle 7 Up
} Add eggs one at a time, beating well after each. Add vanilla and stir. Add flour and stir in with a spoon, then add 7 Up and beat until smooth.

Pour into a greased and floured Bundt pan.
Bake in a 350⁰ oven for 1 hour.

APPLESAUCE CAKE

3 1/2 cups flour
1/4 tsp. cinnamon
1/4 tsp. nutmeg
1/4 tsp. allspice
} Mix together in a medium bowl.

2 cups sugar
1 cup butter
2 eggs
1 tsp. vanilla
} Cream sugar and butter in a large bowl with an electric mixer. Add eggs and vanilla. Mix well.

2 cups applesauce
2 tsp. baking soda
} Mix together in a small bowl.

2 cups raisins
2 cups chopped pecans

Mix flour and applesauce alternately into creamed mixture. Mixing well. Add raisins and pecans and stir well. Pour into a greased and floured Bundt pan. Bake in a 300⁰ oven for 1 hour.

156

BETTER THAN ALMOST ANYTHING CAKE

1 German chocolate cake mix } Bake according to directions on the box.

1 (5 ounce) can condensed milk
1 jar caramel ice cream topping

While cake is still warm, poke holes in the cake with the handle of a wooden spoon. Pour condensed milk over the cake. Next, top with caramel topping. Cool completely. Cover and refrigerate if not serving immediately.

1 (12 ounce) carton cool whip
1 bag toffee bits

When ready to serve, top with cool whip and toffee bits.

BUTTERMILK POUND CAKE

1 cup shortening
3 cups sugar
6 eggs (crack one at a time into a cup, then drop into batter as directed)
3 cups flour
1/2 tsp. salt
1 tsp. vanilla
1 cup buttermilk
1/8 tsp. baking soda

Cream shortening and sugar in a large bowl with electric mixer. Add eggs, one at a time, mixing well. Combine flour and salt in a medium bowl and set aside. Combine vanilla, buttermilk and soda in a small bowl. Add flour and liquid alternately to the creamed mixture and mix well after each addition.

Grease and flour a large Bundt pan. Pour batter into the bundt pan and bake in a 350⁰ oven for 1 hour. Remove pan from oven and let the cake cool in the pan for 5 minutes. Remove cake from pan onto a serving plate. Pour warm glaze over the top.

GLAZE:

1 cup sugar
1/2 cup water
1 tsp. coconut or lemon flavoring

Boil sugar and water in a medium saucepan for 1 minute. Remove from heat and add flavoring. Stir well.

157

CHERRY PUDDING CAKE

1 cup sugar
1 tsp. baking soda
1 cup flour
1 tsp. salt

Combine in a large bowl and make a "well" in the center.

1 cup canned, pitted cherries
    with juice
1 egg, well beaten
1 TBSP butter, melted
1 cup chopped pecans

Mix cherries, egg and butter together in a medium bowl and pour into the well of the dry mixture. Stir to combine. Add pecans and mix well.

SAUCE:
1/2 cup brown sugar
2 TBSP flour
1/2 cup warm water
1 TBSP butter, melted
1 tsp. vanilla

Combine sugar and flour in a medium saucepan. Add warm water and butter. Stir to combine. Cook on low heat until thick. Remove from heat, add vanilla and mix well. Set aside.

Grease a 7 1/2" x 12" x 2" baking dish and pour the cake batter into the dish.
Bake in a 350⁰ oven for 35 minutes.
Pour sauce over the cake while it is still warm.
Serve with whipped cream, if desired.

COCA COLA CHOCOLATE CAKE

2 cups sugar } Mix together with a whisk in a
2 cups flour } large bowl.

1/2 cup butter ⎫ Combine in a medium saucepan
1/2 cup shortening ⎬ and bring to a boil. Remove from
3 TBSP cocoa ⎬ heat and add to the dry ingredients.
1 cup Coca Cola ⎭ Stir well.

1/2 cup buttermilk ⎫
1 tsp. baking soda ⎬ Reserve marshmallows and add
1 tsp. vanilla ⎬ remaining ingredients to batter.
2 eggs, beaten ⎬ Beat well. Fold in marshmallows.
1 1/2 cups small marshmallows ⎭

Pour into a greased 9" x 13" x 2" baking pan.
Bake in a 350⁰ oven for 40 minutes.

CREAM CHEESE POUND CAKE

DO NOT PRE-HEAT OVEN

1 cup margarine ⎫
1/2 cup butter ⎬
1 (8 ounce) pkg. cream cheese ⎬ In a large bowl cream together
2 tsp. vanilla ⎬ margarine, butter, cream cheese and
3 cups sugar ⎬ sugar with an electric mixer. Add
6 large eggs (crack one at a time ⎬ eggs, one at a time, beating well
        into a cup, then ⎬ after each addition. Add vanilla and
        drop into batter ⎬ stir. Add flour and mix well.
        as directed) ⎬
3 cups cake flour (see note below) ⎭

Pour into a greased and floured Bundt pan.
Place in COLD oven. Turn on oven to 275⁰ and bake for 2 1/2 hours.
DO NOT OPEN OVEN DOOR.

NOTE: To use regular flour instead of cake flour, remove 2 TBSP flour from
each cup measured.

DR PEPPER CHOCOLATE CAKE

1 German Chocolate cake mix
1 (3 ounce) pkg. jello instant
          vanilla pudding mix
3/4 cup cooking oil
4 large eggs (crack one at a time
          into a cup, then
          drop into batter
          as directed)
1 (12 ounce) can Dr Pepper

In a large bowl, blend cake mix and pudding mix. Add oil and mix well. Add eggs, one at a time, mixing after each addition. Add Dr Pepper and stir well.

FROSTING:
1 (8 ounce) pkg. cream cheese
1/2 cup butter
1/4 cup cocoa
3 cups powdered sugar
1 tsp. vanilla
1 cup chopped pecans

In a medium bowl, cream cheese and butter. Add cocoa and vanilla. Add in sugar and mix well. Add pecans. Mix well.

Divide batter into two 9" round greased cake pans.
Bake in a 325⁰ oven for 35 minutes.

Remove pans from oven and let cake rest in pans for 5 minutes. Remove cakes from pans and place on cooling racks to cool completely.
Place one cake layer on a large cake plate and spread enough frosting to cover top. Stack second cake layer on top and spread it with the remaining frosting. Keep covered until ready to serve.

DUMP CAKE

1 (20 ounce) can crushed
  pineapple
1 (21 ounce) can strawberry pie
  filling
1 yellow cake mix
1/2 cup butter
1/2 cup chopped pecans

Mix pineapple and pie filling in a medium bowl, then spread in a 9" x 13" x 2" baking dish. Sprinkle cake mix evenly over the top and dot with pats of butter. Top with chopped pecans.

Bake in a 350⁰ oven for 45 minutes.
Remove from oven and cool in the pan.
To serve, cut in squares and top with whipped cream.

FUDGE CAKE

Preheat oven to 325⁰

1 1/2 cups butter
3 cups sugar
5 eggs

In a large bowl, using an electric mixer, cream butter and sugar together. Add eggs one at a time, beating well after each addition.

3 cups flour
1/2 tsp. baking powder
1/2 tsp. salt
4 heaping TBSP cocoa

Mix together with a whisk in a medium bowl.

1 cup milk
1 tsp. vanilla extract

Stir vanilla into milk. Add alternately with dry mixture to creamed mixture. Beat well.

ICING: (Prepare while cake is
        cooling.)
2 cups sugar
1 (5 ounce) can condensed milk
12 large marshmallows
1/2 cup butter
1 (1 1/2 ounce) pkg. chocolate
        chips
1 tsp. vanilla

Mix sugar, milk and marshmallows in a large saucepan and heat on medium, stirring constantly. Boil 6 minutes. Remove from heat and add remaining ingredients. Stir to melt chips and set aside.

Pour cake batter into a greased and floured Bundt pan.
Bake in a pre-heated 325⁰ oven for 1 hour. Remove from oven and cool in pan for 5 minutes, then remove the cake from the pan onto serving plate. Spread icing over the cooled cake.

GRANDMOTHER'S CHOCOLATE CAKE

I prefer using strong coffee for the liquid.

2 cups flour
2 cups sugar
1/2 cup cocoa
1 tsp. soda
1 tsp. cinnamon
1 tsp. allspice
1/2 tsp. cloves
1 cup shortening
4 eggs
1 cup cold brewed coffee (or) milk
(or) buttermilk
1 tsp. vanilla extract

In a large bowl, combine dry ingredients with a whisk. Add remaining ingredients and stir with a large spoon just enough to dampen flour. Using an electric mixer, beat until light brown in color.

Pour batter into a greased 9" x 14" x 2 1/2" baking pan.
Bake in a 350⁰ oven for 25 to 30 minutes or until toothpick comes out clean.
DO NOT OVER BAKE. The cake will feel sticky on top.
Ice, if desired.

LOW CALORIE CHEESE CAKE

1 cup low-fat milk
3/4 cup sugar
2 eggs, separated, reserve whites
(check page 18)
2 envelopes unflavored gelatin
2 TBSP lemon juice
2 tsp. grated lemon rind

Mix together milk, sugar, egg yolks only, and gelatin in a medium saucepan and cook on medium-low heat just until gelatin is dissolved. Remove from heat, add lemon juice and rind, stir well. Return to heat and let cook until slightly thickened. Remove from heat.

1 (16 ounce) carton low calorie
cottage cheese
1 (2.60 ounce) Dream Whip

In a medium bowl, beat egg whites until slightly stiff. In a medium bowl, mix Dream Whip according to package directions. Add egg whites, dream whip, and cottage cheese to cooked mixture and mix thoroughly. Pour into a loaf pan.

1/2 cup graham cracker crumbs
1 tsp. cinnamon
1 tsp. vanilla extract

In a small bowl, mix together and sprinkle on top of cake.

Cover and chill for several hours or overnight.
Serve plain or with fresh strawberries.

OATMEAL CAKE

1 1/4 cups boiling water
1 cup regular oats

} Mix together in a medium bowl and let soak for about 30 minutes.

1 cup sugar
1 cup brown sugar
1/2 cup shortening
2 eggs, beaten
1 tsp. vanilla
1 1/3 cups flour
1 tsp. baking soda
1/2 tsp. salt
1/2 tsp. cinnamon
1/2 tsp. nutmeg

In a large bowl, mix together well.
Add oats and mix again.
Spray a 9" x 13" x 2" baking pan with cooking spray. Pour in batter.

Bake in a 325⁰ oven for 45 minutes.
Remove cake from oven and ice immediately following directions below.

ICING:
1/4 cup butter
1 cup brown sugar
1 egg, beaten
1 can Angel Flake coconut
1 cup chopped pecans

In a medium bowl, mix together and spread on top of cake. Place cake in oven under the broiler and broil until brown on top.
DO NOT put the cake too close to broiler or the topping will not get done enough before it browns.

ONE-TWO-THREE-FOUR CAKE

1 cup butter
2 cups sugar
4 eggs, separated (check page 18)
1 tsp. lemon extract

} In a large bowl, cream butter and sugar until creamy. In a small bowl, beat egg yolks. Add beaten egg yolks and lemon extract to the creamed mixture. Beat well.

3 cups flour
3 tsp. baking powder
1/4 tsp. salt

} Mix together in a medium bowl.

1 cup milk

} Add to the creamed mixture alternately with the flour mixture.

In a medium bowl, beat egg whites until stiff and fold into batter.
Pour into a 9" x 13" x 2" greased baking dish.
Bake in a 375^0 oven for 30 minutes.

PECAN PIE MUFFINS

Preheat oven to 350^0
Grease 3 (12 cup) mini-muffin tins

1 cup brown sugar
1/2 cup flour
2 eggs, slightly beaten
2/3 cup butter, melted
1 cup chopped pecans
1/2 tsp. salt
1 tsp. vanilla

} Mix all ingredients in a large bowl with a wooden spoon.

Fill each muffin cup 2/3 full (do not over fill).
Bake in a pre-heated 350^0 oven for 12 to 15 minutes.
Makes 2 1/2 to 3 dozen muffins.

PRUNE CAKE

1 1/2 cups sugar
1 cup cooking oil
3 eggs, well beaten
1 cup buttermilk
1 cup cooked prunes, chopped

In a large bowl, using an electric mixer, combine sugar and oil. Add eggs and mix slowly. Beat in buttermilk, then prunes.

2 cups flour
1 tsp. baking soda
1/2 tsp. salt
1 tsp. cinnamon
1 tsp. cloves
1 tsp. nutmeg
1 tsp. allspice
1 cup chopped pecans

In a medium bowl, stir together dry ingredients with a whisk. Stir into batter and mix well. Add pecans, stirring again well.

FROSTING:
1 (16 ounce) box powdered sugar
4 TBSP butter, melted
3 to 4 TBSP cream (or)
                    half & half

Mix together in a medium bowl. Set aside.

Grease and flour a 9" x 13" x 2" baking pan. Pour the cake batter into the pan. Bake in a 350^0 oven for 40 minutes. Test the center of the cake with a toothpick to see if it is done. If the toothpick comes out clean, the cake is done. If it is not done, cook another 10 minutes or until done.
Cool before frosting.

Can't Boil Water #30: It is best to cook prunes the day before using them in a cake recipe so the prunes can set in their own juice overnight in the refrigerator.

STRAWBERRY CAKE

1 box white cake mix
1/2 cup water
2/3 cup cooking oil
4 eggs, beaten
1 (3 ounce) pkg. strawberry jello
1 large box frozen strawberries,
      thawed then divided

In a large bowl, combine cake mix, water and oil with an electric mixer. Blend in eggs. Add jello and 1/2 box thawed strawberries. Pour batter evenly into two greased and floured 9" round cake pans.

ICING:
1/2 cup butter
1 pound box powdered sugar

In a medium bowl, combine well and add remaining strawberries. Blend until creamy, then set aside.

Bake cake in a 350⁰ oven for 35 to 40 minutes.

Bake cake in a 350^0 oven for 35 to 40 minutes.
Remove pans from oven and let rest 5 minutes. Remove cakes from pans onto cooling racks.
When cool, place one cake layer on a cake plate. Spread about half the icing on top of the cake layer. Place remaining cake layer on top and spread it with the remaining icing.
If not serving immediately, cover and refrigerate.

Can't Boil Water #31: If the frozen strawberries are sugar free, you may want to thaw the night before, in a covered container, with a little sugar sprinkled over the strawberries.

PIES

PIE CRUST

Makes 3 single crusts.

3 cups sifted flour
1 tsp. salt
1 cup shortening
4 TBSP water
1 TBSP vinegar
1 egg, beaten

} Place flour and salt into a medium size bowl. Cut in shortening with a pastry cutter. In a small bowl, mix water, vinegar and egg together, then pour into dry mixture. Stir enough to dampen flour.

Place on a floured pastry cloth and knead to blend. Divide into 3 parts. Roll out to use immediately or place each part into separate ziploc bags and store in refrigerator.

GRAHAM CRACKER PIE CRUST

1 1/2 cups graham cracker crumbs
1/4 cup sugar
1/2 cup butter, melted

} In a medium bowl, mix well.

Press firmly into a buttered 9" pie pan. Chill crust in the refrigerator until set (about 45 minutes). When ready to use, bake in a 375⁰ oven for 12 minutes.

MERINGUE

Basic Recipe - 1 crust pie

2 or 3 egg whites (check page 18)
1 tsp. extract *
1/8 tsp. cream of tartar
1/4 cup sugar

} Using an electric mixer on high speed, beat egg whites, extract and cream of tartar together until soft peaks form. Gradually add sugar, beating until stiff. Spread on top of cream pie filling.

Bake in a 350⁰ oven for 15 minutes or until golden.

* Choose extract according to type of pie. For example use lemon extract for a lemon pie and vanilla extract for an apple pie.

HINT: To test meringue, rub a small amount between thumb and finger. If it feels gritty, beat longer.

APPLE COBBLER

3 (20 ounce) cans apple pie filling
3/4 cup brown sugar
1 1/2 tsp. cinnamon   Mix together in a large bowl.
2/3 cup white cooking wine
1 cup water

Pie dough to equal 3 crusts

Lightly butter a 9" x 13" x 2" glass ovenproof dish.
On a lightly floured pastry cloth, roll 2/3 of the dough into a large rectangle
that will fit into the dish and hang over the sides. Loosely roll the dough up on
the rolling pin. Holding it in place, transfer dough to pan and unroll starting
at one end. Press dough into pan leaving dough hanging over the sides. Pour
mixture onto dough. Roll out remaining dough. Using a 3" apple shaped cookie
cutter, cut out one "apple" from center of dough, reserving the cut out piece.
Loosely roll dough around rolling pin and transfer to top of apple mixture.
Fold the dough that is around edges toward the inside of the top loosely. Place
the cut out "apple" dough on top, off center of the open cutout hole.
Bake in a 375^0 oven for 45 minutes or until golden.

APPLE DUMPLINGS

2 (8 count) cans crescent rolls
        (16 rolls)   Wash, peel, core and cut apples into
2 medium size Gala apples   8 sections each. Roll each slice in a
                                     crescent roll and place in a
                                     9" x 13" x 2" baking dish.

1 cup butter, melted
1 1/4 cups sugar   Combine and pour over the apple
1 tsp. vanilla extract   rolls.

1/2 cup Mountain Dew (or)
        Jarritos Pineapple pop   Pour soda pop over the rolls and
1 1/2 tsp. cinnamon   sprinkle with cinnamon.

Bake in a 350^0 oven for 40 minutes.
DO NOT over bake.

HINT: Jarritos can be found in the Mexican Food Section or in the soft drink
section of the grocery store.

APRICOT STRUDEL

1 cup butter, softened
1 (8 ounce) pkg. cream cheese
2 1/4 cups flour

In a medium bowl, cream the butter and the cream cheese together until smooth. Measure flour into a medium bowl and stir with a whisk. Add flour to the butter mixture and stir until mixture forms smooth ball. Wrap in plastic wrap and chill 3 to 4 hours or overnight.

1/2 cup apricot preserves
1 (15 ounce) pkg. white raisins
1 (4 ounce) pkg. flaked coconut
2 cups chopped pecans

In a small bowl, stir apricot preserves (this softens the preserves.) Combine remaining ingredients in another medium bowl.

Divide dough into 4 equal parts. On a floured pastry cloth, roll each part into a 14" x 16" rectangle. Divide apricot preserves evenly on each piece and spread over dough. Sprinkle coconut mixture evenly over each piece then roll each rectangle into a jelly roll (log) beginning on the long side. Turn ends under. Place on an ungreased baking sheet and bake in a 350⁰ oven for 40 minutes. Remove from oven and let cool. Cover and chill in refrigerator several hours (or wrap in plastic wrap and freeze).
To serve, cut in 1/4" slices.

Can't Boil Water #32: For a different flavor in a pie crust, add 1 TBSP finely chopped pecans or walnuts; 1 tsp. lemon rind or lemon flavoring; 1/4 tsp. cinnamon or apple pie spices. Experiment! ! !

BASIC CRÊPES

4 large eggs
1 cup flour
1/2 cup milk
1/2 cup water
3 TBSP butter, melted
1 TBSP sugar
1/2 tsp. salt

} Whisk together in a large bowl. Cover and chill 1 hour.

Heat a lightly greased 8" non-stick skillet on medium heat until skillet is hot. Pour 2 TBSP batter into skillet and quickly tilt the skillet in all directions so the batter covers the inside of the bottom of skillet. Cook 2 minutes or until crêpe can be shaken loose from skillet. Turn crepe over and cook about 30 seconds more. Repeat with remaining batter. Stack crêpes between sheets of wax paper until ready to fill.

CHERRY ENCHILADAS

18 to 20 flour tortillas
2 (20 ounce) cans cherry pie
    filling

} Place about 2 TBSP pie filling down center of each tortilla and roll. Place, seam side down, in a 9" x 13" x 2" baking dish.

2 cups water
1 1/2 cups sugar
1 cup butter

} Bring to a boil in a medium saucepan. Pour over enchiladas. Let set a minimum of 2 hours. Refrigerate if letting set overnight.

1 cup pecans
2 TBSP sugar
1/2 tsp. cinnamon

} Mix together and set aside.

Bake in a 350⁰ oven for 20 minutes (30 minutes if cold from refrigerator). Remove from oven and add pecan mixture. Return to oven for 10 minutes.

CHURCH PIE

Graham cracker crust 9" deep dish pie pan	} Prepare crust according to directions on page 167.
1 1/2 pounds cream cheese 3/4 cup sugar 3 eggs 1/4 cup butter, melted 1 tsp. lemon juice Pinch of salt	In a medium bowl, beat cream cheese until light. Add eggs and sugar, then beat until fluffy. Add butter, lemon juice and salt. Stir together well. Pour into pie crust.
TOPPING: 2 cups sour cream 2 TBSP sugar 1 tsp. vanilla extract	Mix together and set aside.

Bake pie in a 375⁰ pre-heated oven for 20 minutes. Remove from oven and increase oven temperature to 450⁰. Spoon the topping onto the top of the pie and return it to the oven to bake for more 5 minutes.
Remove from oven and cool pie. Chill in the refrigerator before serving.
Add fresh, sweet berries, if desired.

FRENCH LEMON CUSTARD PIE

1 pkg. refrigerated pie dough (or) make dough from recipe on page 167	Use 1 crust from the package. Press into a 9" pie plate and flute around the top.
3 eggs, beaten 1 cup sugar 3/4 cup light corn syrup 1/4 cup butter, melted 3 heaping tsp. flour 1/2 tsp. vanilla Juice of 1 lemon	Mix together in a medium bowl, stirring well. Pour into pie shell.

Bake in a 350⁰ oven for 40 minutes.

KEY LIME PIE

1 graham cracker crust (recipe, page 167) or purchase from
grocery store.

1/4 cup boiling water 1 small pkg. sugar free lime jello 2 cartons key lime yogurt 1 (8 ounce) carton cool whip	In a large bowl, dissolve jello in boiling water. Add yogurt and stir well. Fold in cool whip and pour into the crust.

Refrigerate, covered, several hours or overnight.

MILLIONAIRE PIE

2 baked pie crusts
(use 1 pkg. refrigerated dough or recipe on page 167)

2 cups powdered sugar 1/2 cup butter 1/8 tsp. salt 1/4 tsp. vanilla extract	In a medium bowl, cream sugar and butter together. Add salt and vanilla, beating until light and fluffy. Spread mixture evenly into baked crusts. Chill in the refrigerator.
1 cup crushed pineapple, drained 1/2 cup chopped pecans 1 cup whipped cream	In a medium bowl, fold all together and spread over the butter/sugar mixture that is in the pie crusts. Chill in the refrigerator.

Can't Boil Water #33: Unless a recipe specifically
calls for whipped cream, Cool Whip can be
substituted.

MOLASSES PIE

1 unbaked pie crust

} Use recipe on page 167 or half of one package refrigerated pie dough. Place dough into a 9" pie pan. Press the dough into the inside of the bottom and up sides of the pie pan, leaving about 1" over the top. Flute edges.

1 cup sugar
3 TBSP flour
3 eggs, beaten
3 TBSP butter, melted
1 cup molasses
1 tsp. vanilla extract

} In a medium bowl, whisk together sugar and flour. Add remaining ingredients and mix well.

Pour into the unbaked pie crust.
Bake in a 350^0 oven for 1 hour.

NEW BRIDE'S PIE

1 pie crust

} Bake according to directions on page 95.

1 can sweetened condensed milk

} Remove paper from can. Cook in a small saucepan using gently boiling water for 1 hour. Remove can and cool.

2 cups whipped cream

Open can (the mixture will be thick) and spoon into cooled pie crust. Top with whipped cream and refrigerate.

OATMEAL PIE

1 pie crust

} Use recipe on page 167 or half of one package refrigerated pie dough. Press dough into a 9" pie pan and flute edges.

2/3 cup sugar
2/3 cup uncooked oats
1 TBSP brown sugar
2/3 cup butter, melted
2/3 cup light corn syrup
2 eggs, well beaten
1 tsp. vanilla extract

} In a medium bowl, combine sugar, oats and brown sugar. Mix together with a whisk. Add remaining ingredients and mix well.

Pour into the unbaked pie crust.
Bake in a 350⁰ oven for 1 hour.

OAT-APPLE CRISP

5 medium tart apples
2 TBSP lemon juice

} Wash, peel, core and slice apples. Sprinkle with lemon juice (this prevents the apples from turning brown).

1/3 cup brown sugar
1/3 cup sugar
1/2 cup flour
3/4 cup uncooked oats
1/2 cup butter, melted
1/3 cup water

} Arrange sliced apples in a buttered 8" square baking dish. In a medium bowl, combine the sugars, flour and oats. Stir in melted butter. Spread mixture over the apples. Pour water evenly over top.

Bake in a 375⁰ oven for 30 minutes or until apples are tender and top is nicely browned.
Serve warm with ice cream or whipped cream.

PETITE PASTRIES

2 (8 ounce) pkgs. cream cheese 1 cup butter 2 cups flour	In a medium bowl, mix well. Form a ball and seal in a ziploc bag. Chill in the refrigerator.

Pineapple or apricot preserves

Divide dough into small batches. On a floured pastry cloth roll thin, one batch at a time. Cut into 2" squares. Place a spoonful of preserves in the center then bring up pastry corners toward center and seal. Place on a cookie sheet. Bake in a 450⁰ oven for 10 minutes or until light brown.

PINEAPPLE-SOUR CREAM PIE

1 baked 9" pie crust (Can't Boil Water #21)

3/4 cup sugar
1/4 cup flour
1/2 tsp. salt
1 (20 ounce) can crushed
         pineapple undrained
1 cup sour cream
1 TBSP lemon juice
2 eggs, separated (reserve whites)
  (check page 18 for instructions)
	In a large saucepan, combine sugar, flour and salt with a whisk. Stir in pineapple, sour cream and lemon juice. Cook on medium heat, stirring constantly, until mixture thickens and comes to a boil. Cook 2 minutes. Place egg yolks in a small bowl, add a small amount of the hot mixture and stir well. Pour the egg mixture back into hot mixture and cook another 2 minutes.

MERINGUE: Reserved egg whites 1/2 tsp. vanilla extract 1/8 tsp. cream of tartar 1/4 cup sugar	With an electric mixer on high speed, beat egg whites, vanilla and cream of tartar together until mixture forms soft peaks. Gradually add sugar, beating until stiff.

Spoon pineapple mixture into the pie shell, top with meringue.
Bake in a 350⁰ oven for 15 minutes or until meringue is a golden brown.

PUMPKIN PIE

Preheat oven to 325⁰

1 graham cracker crust
1 (9") pie plate

Follow recipe on page 167. Bake crust only 5 minutes. For a different flavor, use chocolate or gingersnap cookies, crushed fine, instead of graham crackers.

3/4 cup packed brown sugar
1 TBSP flour
1 tsp. ginger
1/4 tsp. cloves
1 tsp. cinnamon
2 eggs, beaten
1 (12 ounce) can evaporated milk
1 tsp. vanilla extract
1 (15 ounce) can pumpkin pureé

In a large bowl, mix sugar, flour and spices. In a small bowl, mix eggs, milk and vanilla. Combine both mixtures in the large bowl. Add pumpkin and stir until well blended.

Pour mixture into the pie crust.
Bake in a pre-heated 325⁰ oven for 1 hour or until a knife inserted in the center comes out clean. Remove from oven and cool on a wire rack.

Can't Boil Water #34: For an easy way to crush cookies, crackers, cereal, etc., place into a 1 quart ziploc bag, squeeze as much air out as possible, zip closed and crush with a rolling pin. Turn bag over several times to evenly crush the contents.

RAISIN PIE

Pastry from recipe on page 167

Divide dough into three equal parts. Wrap one part in a ziploc bag and refrigerate for later use. Using the remaining dough, cover one to prevent drying and roll out the third on a lightly floured pastry cloth to a 13" circle. Place the rolled out dough in a 9" pie pan and trim dough to 1/2" beyond rim. Set aside.

3 cups raisins
3/4 cup brown sugar
2 TBSP cornstarch
2 TBSP orange drink powder
1 1/4 cups water
2 TBSP lemon juice
1 cup chopped walnuts
2 TBSP butter

In a large saucepan, combine raisins, brown sugar, cornstarch and the orange drink powder. Stir in water and lemon juice. Cook over medium heat, stirring constantly, until mixture boils and thickens (about 10 minutes). Remove from heat and stir in walnuts.

Pour mixture into prepared pie crust and dot with butter.
Uncover reserved second part of dough and roll out to an 11" circle and place over filling. Trim the edge to 1" beyond the rim. Fold top crust under the bottom crust and flute edge of dough. Cut several steam vents in the top crust.
Bake in a 400⁰ oven for 30 minutes or until crust is golden.

RITZ CRACKER PIE

3 egg whites (check page 18)
1 cup sugar
1 heaping tsp. baking powder
1/8 tsp. salt
20 Ritz crackers, crushed
3/4 cup chopped pecans
} In a medium bowl, beat egg whites until stiff. Gradually add sugar. Add baking powder and salt. Gently fold in cracker crumbs and pecans.

1 cup whipped cream
1/4 cup grated German or Belgium chocolate

Pour the cracker mixture into a well greased 9" pie pan, shaping mixture around the sides.
Bake in 350⁰ oven for 25 minutes. Remove from oven and cool.
Cover with whipped cream and sprinkle chocolate on top.

NOTE: German or Belgium chocolate are sold in solid squares. Belgium chocolate can be purchased at a speciality cooking shop.

SUGAR FREE PUMPKIN PIE

Preheat oven to 425⁰
1 (9" deep dish) pie crust (recipe, page 167)

2 eggs, beaten
1 (15 ounce) can pumpkin pureé
8 ounces evaporated milk
1/2 tsp. salt
1 tsp. cinnamon
1/2 tsp. ginger
1/4 tsp. cloves
8 ounces sugar free syrup
} In a large bowl, mix all ingredients well and pour into prepared pie shell.

Bake in a 425⁰ pre-heated oven for 15 minutes. Reduce heat to 350⁰ and continue baking for 50 minutes or until knife inserted near center comes out clean.

Can't Boil Water #35: If using a purchased pie dough, place on a lightly floured pastry cloth and roll out to 14" diameter so it will be large enough for the deep dish pie plate.

VANILLA CUSTARD

2 cups half & half
1/2 cup sugar*
3 TBSP cornstarch
1/4 tsp. salt
1 tsp. vanilla
1 tsp. butter
2 egg yolks

In the top part of a double boiler, mix dry ingredients together with a whisk. Gradually add half & half, stirring to dissolve cornstarch. Add remaining ingredients.

Add about 1" of water to the bottom part of a double boiler. Put top pan in place. Cook on medium heat (heat may need to be adjusted to prevent water from boiling over the bottom pan), stirring constantly, until mixture is thick and creamy.
The custard may be used for a cream pie or served in cups with whipped cream on top.
*Splenda or an equivalent can be substituted for the sugar.

VINEGAR PIE

Pastry for a 2 crust pie (recipe page 167)

1 1/2 cups sugar
3 1/2 TBSP flour
1/4 tsp. salt
3/4 cup hot water
1/4 cup butter, melted
2 TBSP + 1 tsp. apple cider
vinegar
1/4 tsp. nutmeg

In a medium bowl, mix sugar, flour and salt with a whisk. Add hot water and stir to mix. Add butter and vinegar and stir. Pour into unbaked shell.
Top with crisscross strips of pastry. Trim, leaving 1/2" over edge of pan. Press strips to the edge of the bottom crust, turn under and flute. Sprinkle nutmeg evenly over the top.

Bake in a 400^0 oven for 25 minutes.

COOKIES & CANDY

ALICE COOKIES

1/2 cup shortening
3/4 cup sugar
2 eggs, beaten
1/4 cup milk
1/2 cup coconut
1 cup raisins
1 cup finely chopped pecans

In a large bowl, cream shortening and sugar. Add eggs and milk, beat well. Add coconut, raisins and pecans, beat again.

1 cup oatmeal
1 cup flour
1 tsp. baking powder
1/2 tsp. salt
1 tsp. cinnamon

In a medium bowl, combine all ingredients. Stir into shortening mixture, blend well.

Line a large cookie sheet with parchment paper. Drop dough by teaspoonfuls onto paper, 2" apart.
Bake in a 350⁰ oven for 12 minutes.
Recipe makes about 50 cookies.

CHOCOLATE COVERED PEANUT BUTTER BALLS

1 pound powdered sugar, sifted
1 cup margarine, softened
1 (12 ounce) jar creamy
           peanut butter

} In a large bowl, mix margarine and peanut butter together until creamy. Add powdered sugar and mix well. Roll into nickel size balls. Place on a cookie sheet that has been lined with waxed paper. Cover loosely with waxed paper, then plastic wrap. Freeze overnight.

Dipping chocolate

In a small bowl, melt half of the package of the dipping chocolate according to the package directions. To dip the peanut butter balls, only take a small amount of balls from freezer at one time. Dip each ball into the melted chocolate using a candy dipping wand and place on waxed paper to harden.
Store, covered.
No refrigeration needed.

CHOCOLATE PECAN GRIT BARS

Preheat oven to 350⁰

1 box yellow cake mix
2 eggs, beaten
1/2 cup butter, melted
1 cup cooked grits

} In a large bowl, mix together well. Pour into a well greased 9" x 13" x 2" baking pan.

1 (6 ounce) pkg. chocolate chips
1 cup chopped nuts

} Sprinkle chocolate chips and pecans on top of batter.

1 (8 ounce) pkg. cream cheese
2 eggs, beaten
1 tsp. vanilla extract
1 (16 ounce) pkg. powdered sugar

} In a large bowl, mix cream cheese, eggs and vanilla until creamy. Sift powdered sugar and add, in small portions, to the creamed mixture. Beat until creamy and pour on the top of ingredients in the pan.

Bake in a pre-heated 350⁰ oven for 45 minutes. Remove from oven and let cool for 1 hour and 10 minutes before cutting into squares and serving.

TIP: If you place the cooled pan in the freezer, this will help the bars come out of the pan easier.

CHOW MEIN CANDY

1 large pkg. chow mein noodles
2 (6 ounce) pkgs. butterscotch
     chips
1 cup Spanish peanuts

} In a large heavy saucepan, melt chips on low heat. Add noodles and peanuts. Mix well.

Drop by teaspoon onto waxed paper.
Store in a covered container.

Can't Boil Water #36: To store cookies or candy, cut several pieces of waxed paper the size of the can or box being used for storing. Place one piece of waxed paper on the bottom, then place one layer of goodies on top of the waxed paper, then top with another piece of waxed paper. Continue until the can is full.

COCONUT-PECAN DELIGHT BAR COOKIES

1 1/2 cups baking mix
2 cups brown sugar
4 eggs, slightly beaten
1 cup coconut
1 cup chopped pecans

} In a large bowl, mix all together with a fork. Pour into 9" x 13" x 2" greased baking pan.

Bake in a 350^0 oven for 35 minutes.
Remove pan from oven and let cool completely, then cut into squares and remove from pan.
Store in a covered container.

CREAMY MARSHMALLOW FUDGE

2 1/4 cups sugar
3/4 cup evaporated milk
16 large marshmallows (or) 1 cup
          marshmallow cream
1/4 cup butter
1/4 tsp. salt

} In a large saucepan, cook and stir constantly, over medium heat to a boil (mixture will be bubbling all over the top). Boil 5 minutes and then remove from heat.

1 (6 ounce) pkg. chocolate chips
1 tsp. vanilla extract

} Stir into hot mixture until chocolate is completely melted.

Spread evenly into a buttered 8" square pan. Cool before cutting into squares.

EASY CAKE MIX COOKIES

1 box yellow cake mix*
2 eggs
1/2 cup cooking oil
2 tsp. vanilla extract

} In a large bowl, mix ingredients well with a large spoon. Form into balls a little larger than a quarter and place on waxed paper.

1/2 cup sugar
2 tsp. cinnamon

} Stir together in a small bowl and roll balls in the mixture.

Place balls 2" apart on a cookie sheet.
Bake in a 350⁰ oven for 8 to 10 minutes or until cookies are light golden in color.
DO NOT cook too long, the cookies will harden as they cool.

VARIATIONS: Add one of the following: pecans, raisins, chocolate chips or
              M & M's.
*Can use a chocolate cake mix, If desired.

FORT RICHARDSON BROWNIES

2 cups flour
2 cups sugar

} Combine in a large mixing bowl.

1/2 cup butter
1/2 cup shortening
1 cup strong brewed coffee
1/4 cup dark cocoa, unsweetened

In a medium microwave safe dish, combine and microwave on high for 2 minutes or until just boiling around the top edges. Pour over dry mixture and stir to blend.

1/2 cup buttermilk
2 eggs, beaten
1 tsp. baking soda
1 tsp. vanilla extract

Add ingredients, in order given, to batter. Mixing well after each addition.

FROSTING:
1/2 cup butter
2 TBSP dark cocoa
1/4 cup milk
4 cups powdered sugar, sifted
1 tsp. vanilla extract

In a medium microwave safe bowl, microwave butter, cocoa and milk on high 2 minutes or just until boiling at the edges. Slowly add powdered sugar, stirring until smooth after each addition. Add vanilla and beat until very smooth. Set aside.

Pour cocoa/coffee batter into a well buttered 11" x 17 x 1" jelly roll pan. Bake in a 400° oven for 18 minutes or until brownies test done in the center. DO NOT over bake. Remove from oven and cool in pan. Cool about 20 minutes before frosting.

Can't Boil Water #37: I have a special box that I store the brownies in that is several inches taller than the pan so they can be covered without touching the frosting. Check with your local hardware store or a container store for a box.

GELATIN SUGAR COOKIES

3/4 cup shortening
1/2 cup sugar
1 (3 ounce) pkg. jello (any flavor)
2 eggs, slightly beaten

} In a large bowl, cream shortening and sugar. Add jello and stir well. Add eggs and beat together.

2 1/2 cups flour
1 tsp. baking powder
1 tsp. salt

} In a medium bowl, mix together with a whisk, then blend into creamed mixture

1/4 cup colored sugar

Shape dough into 3/4" balls and place on a greased cookie sheet, 2" apart. Using cooking spray, grease the bottom of a drinking glass, dip glass into the colored sugar then use the glass to flatten the cookie balls, repeat dipping the glass bottom into the colored sugar as you flatten each cookie ball.
Bake in a 400⁰ oven for 8 to 10 minutes or until golden in color.

Can't Boil Water #38: To make colored sugar, pour 1 cup sugar into a pint size jar that has a tight fitting lid. Add 2 drops of liquid food coloring. Screw lid on tight and shake vigorously. To use, pour a small amount into a shallow bowl. Do not pour unused portion back into the jar.

GRAHAM CRACKER COOKIE

1/2 cup butter 1 cup brown sugar	} Combine in a medium saucepan and heat on medium until melted.
1 cup pecans or walnuts 1 pkg. of graham crackers from a graham cracker box	} Add nuts to melted mixture and stir well. Spread mixture on top of each graham cracker.

Place the crackers on an ungreased cookie sheet.
Bake in a 350⁰ oven for 10 minutes.

GROOM'S COOKIE

1/2 cup butter, softened	} In a medium bowl, using an electric mixer, beat butter until creamy.
3/4 cup flour 1/4 cup sugar 1/4 cup cocoa 1/4 tsp. salt 1 tsp. vanilla extract 1 cup finely chopped pecans	} In a small bowl, combine flour, sugar, cocoa and salt, then add to butter. Beat until blended. Add vanilla and pecans and stir with a spoon until blended, forming a dough.
1/4 cup powdered sugar 2 TBSP cocoa	} Sift together in a small bowl and set aside.

Shape dough into 1" balls and place 2" apart on ungreased cookie sheet. Flatten dough slightly with a small spatula.
Bake in a 400⁰ oven for 8 to 10 minutes. Remove from oven and cool slightly in the pan, then sprinkle powdered sugar-cocoa mixture over tops of cookies. Transfer to cooling racks to cool completely. Store covered.

HIGH PROTEIN BARS

2 TBSP butter
2 cups miniature marshmallows
2 TBSP peanut butter

In a large saucepan, melt butter on low. Add marshmallows and stir until melted and mixture is syrupy. Remove from heat and stir in peanut butter.

4 cups high protein cereal
1/2 cup chocolate chips

Stir into peanut butter mixture until chips melt and cereal is coated.

Press into an 8" square pan.
Chill in the refrigerator until firm and then cut into bars.

NOTE: Raisins, cut-up dried apricots, coconut or chopped dates can be substituted for the chocolate chips.

HIP-PADDER BARS

1 (14 ounce) can sweetened
             condensed milk
2 TBSP butter
1 (6 ounce) pkg. chocolate chips

Combine in the top of a double boiler. Check page 6 for double boiler instructions. Cook, stirring, until melted and smooth. Set aside to cool.

1 cup brown sugar
1/2 cup butter
1 egg, beaten
1 1/4 cups flour
1/2 cup regular oats
1 tsp. vanilla extract
1 cup chopped pecans

Cream butter and sugar. Add eggs, mixing well. Blend in flour, oats and vanilla. Stir in pecans. Pat into a greased 9" square pan.

Pour chocolate mixture over the top of the pecan crust mixture and spread evenly.
Bake in a 350⁰ oven for 25 minutes.
DO NOT over bake.

JOE FROGGER COOKIES

7 cups flour, sifted 1 TBSP salt 1 TBSP ginger 1 tsp. cloves 1 tsp. nutmeg 1/2 tsp. allspice	Sift together into a large bowl and set aside.
3/4 cup water 1/4 cup rum	Combine in a small bowl and set aside.
2 cups dark molasses 2 tsp. baking soda	Combine in a small bowl and set aside.
1 cup shortening 2 cups sugar	In an extra large bowl, cream together. Add half the water-rum and mix and blend well . Add half the flour mixture and mix well. Add molasses and stir well. Add half remaining flour and mix well. Add remaining water-rum and mix well. Add remaining flour and mix well.

Chill dough in the refrigerator, covered, several hours. Divide into workable portions and roll out on a lightly floured pastry cloth to 1/4" thickness. Cut with a 4" round cookie cutter. Place 2" apart on a greased cookie sheet. Bake in a 375^0 oven for 12 to 15 minutes.

This recipe takes some time, but is well worth it when you take the first bite.

Can't Boil Water #39: If you don't have any rum, measure 1 tsp. rum extract into a 1 cup measuring cup and add water to 1 cup level.

ORANGE REFRIGERATOR COOKIES

1 cup shortening
1/2 cup brown sugar
1/2 cup sugar
1 egg, slightly beaten
2 TBSP orange juice
1 TBSP orange rind

In a large bowl, cream shortening, then add sugars and beat until creamy. Stir in egg, orange juice and rind. Stir well.

2 3/4 cups flour
1/4 tsp. salt
1/4 tsp. baking soda
1/2 cup chopped nuts

Mix flour, salt and soda together in a medium bowl using a whisk. Add to creamed mixture and stir well. Add nuts, stirring until well combined to form a dough.

Divide dough into two equal parts and roll each part forming a log. Place each log on a piece of waxed paper, cover and roll the log in the waxed paper tucking in ends of paper. Refrigerate several hours until well chilled. Slice thin and place on a cookie sheet. Bake in a 375⁰ oven for 10 minutes.

ORANGE SLICE DREAM BARS

2 1/2 cups flour
2 1/2 tsp. baking powder
1/2 tsp. salt

Combine in a medium bowl and stir with a whisk. Set aside.

1 1/2 cups finely cut-up orange
        slice candy
1 cup coconut

Mix together in a medium bowl. Sprinkle with 1 TBSP flour and mix well to coat candy. Set aside.

3/4 cup butter, softened
2 1/2 cups brown sugar
1 tsp. vanilla extract
3 eggs, slightly beaten

In a large bowl, mix together butter and brown sugar. Add vanilla and eggs. Beat with a large wooden spoon until smooth. Add flour mixture stirring well, then add candy-coconut mixture and combine well.

Spray a 10" x 15" x 1" baking sheet with cooking spray and pour batter into pan and spread evenly over bottom. Bake in a 350⁰ oven for 25 minutes. DO NOT over bake. The bars will firm as they cool. Cut into squares.

Can't Boil Water #40: Easy way to cut bar cookies is to use a pizza cutter. It may be necessary to cut edges with a knife.

PECAN SQUARES

1 box yellow cake mix,
          reserve 2/3 cup
1 egg
1/4 cup butter

} In a medium bowl, beat together well using an electric mixer. Grease a 9"x 13"x 2" baking pan. Spread mixture into the pan and bake in a 350⁰ oven for 15 minutes. Remove from oven and set aside.

FILLING:
1/2 cup butter, melted
reserved 2/3 cup cake mix
1/2 cup brown sugar
4 eggs, slightly beaten
3 TBSP whipping cream
1 1/2 cups light karo syrup
2 tsp. vanilla extract
2 cups chopped pecans

} Mix together in a large bowl using a large spoon. Pour over the cooked crust. Return pan to the oven.

Bake in a 350⁰ oven for 35 minutes.
Remove from oven and cool before cutting into bars.

POTATO CHIP COOKIES

2 cups flour
1 tsp. baking soda
1/2 tsp. salt

} In a medium bowl, mix together with a whisk and set aside.

1 cup shortening
1 cup sugar
1 cup brown sugar
2 eggs, beaten

} Cream shortening and both sugars together. Add eggs and mix well. Add dry ingredients and mix again. Mixture will be dry.

1 tsp. vanilla extract
2 cups crushed potato chips
1 1/2 cups finely chopped pecans

} Add to batter and stir well.

Shape into 3/4" balls and place on a cookie sheet.
Bake in a 350⁰ oven for 10 minutes. Remove from oven and place cookies on cooling racks until cool.

SLICED COOKIES

5 cups flour
1 tsp. baking soda
1 tsp. salt
1 tsp. cinnamon

} In a medium bowl, combine and set aside.

1 1/2 cups butter, melted
1 cup sugar
1 cup brown sugar
3 eggs, well beaten
1 cup chopped pecans

} In a large bowl, cream butter and sugars. Add eggs one at a time stirring well after each addition. Blend in pecans. Add dry ingredients and stir well forming a dough.

Shape into 3" diameter rolls (there will be several rolls) and roll waxed paper around each roll, tucking in ends of paper.. Chill in the refrigerator several hours or overnight. Slice thin and place on cookie sheets.
Bake in a 425⁰ oven for 10 minutes or until lightly browned. Remove cookies from oven and let cool on cooling racks.

TOFFEE CRUNCH COOKIES

1 1/2 cups flour
1/2 tsp. salt
1/2 tsp. baking soda

} Combine in a medium bowl and stir together using a whisk.

1/2 cup butter
3/4 cup packed brown sugar
1 egg, slightly beaten
1 tsp. vanilla extract

} Cream together in a large bowl until smooth and creamy. Stir in dry ingredients.

1 cup finely chopped toffee
            candy bars
1/3 cup chopped pecans

} Blend into batter, stirring well.

Drop by TBSP, 2" apart, onto greased baking sheets.
Bake in a 350⁰ oven for 9 to 13 minutes or until golden.

Can't Boil Water #41: Use parchment paper (found at grocery store) to line cookie sheets. No need to grease pans & cookies bake much better using the parchment paper.

EASY MEASURES

MEASURE	EQUALS
Teaspoons	
under 1/8 tsp.	Dash or pinch
1 1/2 tsp.	1/2 TBSP
3 tsp.	1 TBSP
Tablespoons	
1 TBSP	3 tsp.
4 TBSP	1/4 cup
5 1/3 TBSP	1/3 cup
8 TBSP	1/2 cup
10 2/3 TBSP	2/3 cup
16 TBSP	1 cup
Cups	
1/4 cup	4 TBSP
1/3 cup	5 1/3 TBSP
1/2 cup	8 TBSP
1/2 cup	1/4 pint
2/3 cup	10 2/3 TBSP
1 cup	16 TBSP
1 cup	1/2 pint
2 cups	1 pint
4 cups	1 quart
Liquid Measures	
2 TBSP	1 fluid ounce
3 TBSP	1 jigger
1/4 cup	2 fluid ounces
1/2 cup	4 fluid ounces
1 cup	8 fluid ounces

In A Pinch

RECIPE CALLS FOR

SUBSTITUTE

RECIPE CALLS FOR	SUBSTITUTE
1 square unsweetened chocolate	3 TBSP unsweetened cocoa powder + 1 TBSP butter
1 cup cake flour	1 cup less 2 TBSP all-purpose flour
2 TBSP flour (for thickening)	1 TBSP cornstarch
1 cup corn syrup	1 cup sugar + 1/4 cup addition liquid used in recipe
1 cup milk	1/2 cup evaporated milk + 1/2 cup water
1 cup buttermilk or sour milk	1 TBSP vinegar or lemon juice + enough milk to equal 1 cup
1 cup sour cream (for baking)	1 cup plain yogurt
1 cup firmly packed brown sugar	1 cup sugar + 2 TBSP molasses
1 tsp lemon juice	1/4 tsp vinegar (not balsamic)
1/4 cup chopped onion	1 TBSP instant minced onion
1 clove garlic	1/4 tsp garlic powder
2 cups tomato sauce	3/4 cup tomato paste + 1 cup water
1 TBSP prepared mustard	1 tsp dry mustard + 1 TBSP water

CAN'T BOIL WATER

APPETIZERS & BEVERAGES

Appetizers

Baked Brie with Raisin Sauce 19
Basic Sour Cream Dip 20
Biscuit Mix Sausage Balls 20
Caramel Popcorn Crunch 21
Cheese & Olive Tea Sandwiches 21
Cheese-Nut Ball 23
Cheese Appetizer Cookie 22
Cheese Ball 22
Cheese Dainties 23
Chili Cheese Log 24
Chutney Cheese Spread 24
Cucumber Sandwich Spread 25
Curried Egg Sandwiches 25
Dill Dip 26
Egg Salad Sandwich Filling 26
Fruit Dip 27
Garlic Cheese Ball 27
Grape Wienies 28
Ham & Devils 28
Latin Devils 29
Layered Mexican Dip 29

Mexican Fudge 30
Oyster Crackers 30
Pimento Cheese 31
Popcorn Scramble 31
Puppy Chow 32
Red Devil Balls 32
Salmon Spread 33
Sausage Roll 33
Spinach Dip 34
Spinach Pimento Dip 34
Tuna Paté 35
Tuti-Fruiti 35
Vegetable Dip 36
Yummy Caramel Dip 36

Beverages

Cranberry Punch 37
Holiday Punch 38
Orange Julep 38
Peach Punch 39
Percolator Punch 39
Spiced Tea 40
Spiced Tea Mix (no sugar) 40
Tea Syrup 41
Vegetable Juice Cocktails 41
Watermelon Cooler 42

BREADS

Anadama Bread 73
Apricot-Raisin Bread 74
Baking Mix Biscuits 74
Banana Tea Bread 75
Bread Muffins 75
Buttermilk Baking Mix 76
Buttermilk Oatmeal Rolls 76
Cabbage Patch Bread 77
Cheese & Garlic Bread 78
Cheese Bread Sticks 78
Cheese Crumb Muffins 79
Cheese Pinwheel Rolls 79
Cheesy Chip Rolls 80
Cornmeal-Cheddar Muffins 80
Energy Bars 81
Irish Soda Bread 82
Mexican Cornbread 82
Oatmeal Hurry-ups 83
Popovers 83
Puff Ball Coffee Cake 84
Pumpkin Loaf Bread 84
Shortcake Biscuits 85
Soda Pop Biscuits 85
Sopapillas 86
Sour Cream Bread 86
Spoon Rolls 87
Three for One 87
Tomato Bread 88
Whole Wheat Pizza Crust 89
Yeast Cornbread 90

BREAKFAST

Bacon Wrapped Baked Eggs 7
Baked French Toast 8
Breakfast Pie 9
Breakfast Pizza 10
Brunch Huevos Rancheros 11
Buffet Eggs 12
Christmas Brunch Casserole 12
French Toast Waffles 13
Molasses Breakfast Bar 13
Oatmeal Supreme 15
Omelet In A Bag 14
Pancakes 16
Surprise Poached Eggs 16

CAN'T BOIL WATER TIPS

#1 7 - Custard cups
#2 8 - How to melt butter in the microwave
#3 10 - How to test if an egg dish is done
#4 12 - Temperature to cook eggs
#5 13 - How to measure brown sugar
#6 15 - How to toast nuts in the oven
#7 22 - Old English Cheese tip
#8 24 - Keep hands from sticking when molding cheese
#9 24 - Substitution for chives
#10 25 - How to boil eggs
#11 26 - Bread tips for egg salad sandwiches
#12 35 - Preparation for jello mold
#13 37 - Testing spice-water mixture strength

#14 46 - Salad oil vs. cooking oil, olive oil & peanut oil
#15 64 - Chicken stock substitute
#16 73 - Yeast tips
#17 74 - Browning biscuits
#18 82 - Cooking cornbread in an iron skillet
#19 86 - Deep frying
#20 90 - How to scald milk
#21 95 - Baking pie crust without ingredients
#22 98 - Substitute for tart pan
#23 99 - How to test if potatoes are done
#24 103 - How to test if vegetables are done using a fork
#25 116 - How to toast nuts in a skillet
#26 129 - How to test chicken to see if it is done
#27 132 - How to cook frozen chicken breasts
#28 141 - Substitute for Magi seasoning
#29 155 - To grease and flour a pan
#30 165 - Cooking prunes or any dried fruit
#31 166 - Strawberry tip for cakes
#32 169 - Enhancing pie crust by adding flavors
#33 172 - Substitute for whipping cream
#34 176 - How to crush cookies or crackers
#35 178 - How to prepare purchased pie dough for pies
#36 183 - How to store cookies or candy
#37 185 - How to store brownies
#38 186 - How to make colored sugar
#39 189 - How to use Rum extract
#40 190 - Easy way to cut bar cookies
#41 192 - How to use parchment paper

CASSEROLES

Asparagus Casserole 113
Au Gratin Potato Casserole 113
Baked Pasta Casserole 114
Baked Squash Casserole 115
Cabbage Roll Casserole 115
Chicken Noodle Casserole 116
Corn & Pea Casserole 117
Corn Casserole 117
Five Can Casserole 118
Five Soup Casserole 118
Fruit Casserole 119
Grits Casserole 119
Italian Green Bean Casserole 120
Oriental Casserole 120
Spinach Casserole 121
Sweet Potato Casserole 121
Tuna Casserole with Lemon Mustard Sauce 122
Vegetable Casserole 123
Wall's Broccoli Casserole 123
What The Dickens? Sweet Potato Crunch 124

COOKING TIPS

Baking Tips 72
Cooking Terms 18
Easy Measures 193
How to 'season' a cast iron skillet 207
In A Pinch 194
Pan Sizes 6
Salad Tips 44
Spices & Herbs General Guideline 126
Vegetable & Fruit Tips 92

DESSERTS

Cakes

7 Up Cake 156
Applesauce Cake 156
Better Than Almost Anything Cake 157
Buttermilk Pound Cake 157
Cherry Pudding Cake 158
Coca Cola Chocolate Cake 159
Cream Cheese Pound Cake 159
Dr Pepper Chocolate Cake 160
Dump Cake 161
Fudge Cake 161
Grandmother's Chocolate Cake 162
Low Calorie Cheese Cake 162
Mixture to Grease Pans 155
Oatmeal Cake 163
One-Two-Three-Four Cake 164
Pecan Pie Muffins 164
Prune Cake 165
Strawberry Cake 166

Cookies & Candy

Alice Cookies 181
Chocolate Covered Peanut Butter Balls 182
Chocolate Pecan Grit Bars 182
Chow Mein Candy 183
Coconut-Pecan Delight Bar Cookies 183
Creamy Marshmallow Fudge 184
Easy Cake Mix Cookies 184
Fort Richardson Brownies 185
Gelatin Sugar Cookies 186
Graham Cracker Cookie 187
Groom's Cookie 187

High Protein Bars 188
Hip-Padder Bars 188
Joe Frogger Cookies 189
Orange Refrigerator Cookies 190
Orange Slice Dream Bars 190
Pecan Squares 191
Potato Chip Cookies 191
Sliced Cookies 192
Toffee Crunch Cookies 192

Pies

Apple Cobbler 168
Apple Dumplings 168
Apple Strudel 169
Basic Crêpes 170
Cherry Enchiladas 170
Church Pie 171
French Lemon Custard Pie 171
Graham Cracker Pie Crust 167
Key Lime Pie 172
Meringue 167
Millionaire Pie 172
Molasses Pie 173
New Bride's Pie 173
Oat-Apple Crisp 174
Oatmeal Pie 174
Petite Pastries 175
Pie Crust 167
Pineapple-Sour Cream Pie 175
Pumpkin Pie 176
Raisin Pie 177
Ritz Cracker Pie 178
Sugar Free Pumpkin Pie 178
Vanilla Custard 179
Vinegar Pie 179

MAIN DISHES

BBQ Hamburger Mix 127
Beef Stroganoff 128
Beer Can Grilled Chicken 129
Burger-Squash Quiche 130
Cheeseburger Mini Meatloaf's 131
Chicken Chow Mein 131
Chicken Spaghetti 133
Chicken with Stuffing 132
Chili-Tamale Bake 134
Chuck Wagon Chili 134
Chuck Wagon Skillet 135
Crêpe Burritos 135
Crock-Pot BBQ Beef 136
Garden Tuna Spaghetti 137
Glazed Baked Ham 138
Great BBQ Sauce 138
Hot Meat Sandwich 139
Impossible Taco Pie 139
Irish Stew with Dumplings 140
Lip Smacking BBQ Ribs 140
Lunch Meat and Bean Combo 141
Main Dish Steamed Cabbage 141
Meal in a Pot 142
Mexican Pie 143
Mock Enchiladas 144
Pan Pizza 144
Patio Supper 145
Pizza Pie 145
Ranch BBQ Muffins 146
Salami Treat 147
Salmon Alaska 147
Salmon Quesadillas 148
Skillet Corned Beef and Cabbage 148

Sour Cream Enchiladas 149
Spaghetti & Meatballs 149
Spaghetti with Meat Sauce 150
Spanish Rice with Vienna Sausage 150
Swiss Steak with Rice 151
Tuna with Mushroom Sauce on Toast 151
Veggie-Burger Pizza 152
Very Easy Pizza Sauce 152

SALADS & SOUPS

Salads

Apricot Nut Chicken Salad 45
Argyle Salad 45
Baked Fruit Medley 46
Cabbage Salad 46
Cherry Coke Salad 47
Chicken Salad 47
Cookie Salad 48
Cranberry Fluff 48
Cranberry Salad 49
Creamy Cherry Jello Salad 49
Egg Salad 50
Frito Salad 50
Frozen Cranberry Salad 51
Frozen Fruit Salad 51
Frozen Yogurt Salad 52
Fruit Salad Dressing 52
Grape Salad 53
Hot German Potato Salad 53
Indian Slaw 54
Lime-Sour Cream Salad 54

Luncheon Salad 55
My Favorite Tuna Salad 55
Old Fashioned Cole Slaw 56
Patton's Fruit Salad 56
Pistachio Salad 57
Ranch Picnic Potato Salad 57
Rickshaw Salad 58
Southwestern Cornbread Salad 59
Spicy Cole Slaw 60
Spinach Salad 60
Strawberry Jello Salad 61
Three Bean Salad 61
Twenty-Four Hour Fruit Salad 62
Whipped Lime Jello Salad 62
Wilted Lettuce Salad 63
Zip Salad 63

Soups

Canadian Cheese Soup 64
Cheesy Cream of Squash Soup 65
Cheesy Potato Soup 66
Chicken Tortilla Soup 66
Four Bean Salsa Soup 67
King Ranch Soup 67
Old Fashioned Soup 68
Potato Soup Mix in a Jar 68
Santa Fe Soup 69
Ultimate Baked Potato Soup 69

VEGETABLES

Bacon Wrapped Corn on the Cob 93
Baked Cauliflower 93
Baked Spinach 94
Basic Quiche Recipe 95
Cheddar Baked Potatoes 96
Cheese Puffs for Two 97
Cheesy Pizza Potatoes 97
Cheesy Tomato Tart 98
Chef-Baked Cheese Potatoes 99
Cottage Cheese Scalloped Potatoes 100
Cream Cheese Corn 100
Dijon Potatoes 101
Eggplant Pie 101
Ginger Asparagus 102
Holiday Green Beans 102
Maple Syrup Sweet Potatoes 103
Okra Croquettes 104
Oven Baked Zucchini Chips 104
Oven Rice 105
Potatoes Romanoff 106
Potato Puff 105
Rice and Carrots 106
Scalloped Cider Potatoes 107
Scalloped Yams with Apricots 107
Sour Cream Potatoes with Olives 108
Special Candied Sweet Potatoes 108
Squash Croquettes 109
Western Corn Soufflé 109
Zucchini Fries 110

HOW TO 'SEASON'
A
CAST IRON SKILLET

Wash skillet in hot, soapy water. Rinse thoroughly and dry completely. Apply a thin coating of melted shortening or vegetable oil (do not use butter or margarine, it will burn) with a paper towel to the inside of the skillet. Preheat oven to 350 degrees. Place foil on a cookie sheet and place the cookie sheet on bottom rack of oven. This will catch the drippings from the skillet. Place skillet UPSIDE DOWN on top oven rack. Bake in oven for one hour. Turn oven off. DO NOT OPEN. Allow skillet to cool down in oven (several hours). There may be a film on your cookware, this comes off after use.

Printed in the United States
78037LV00001B/13-18